Women I Want to Grow Old With

Grow Old Together with Courage, Health, and Attitude!

By

Diane Gage Lofgren
and
Margaret Bhola

D0950976

Dedication

To all the women we want to grow old with—past, present, and future!

Acknowledgements

Our sincere gratitude to the many women and friends we spoke with to write this book. Their insights and stories will assist us all in making and keeping female friends—and to be the types of women others want to grow old with. Special appreciation goes to Lolma Olson for sharing the term "intention holders" with us. It perfectly describes the girlfriends who, like her, hold our best intentions in their hearts.

Love to our husbands, Matt and Ravi, and our adult children, Kevin, Amanda, Elizabeth, Paul, and MargE, for their encouragement throughout the process. Special thanks to Noonie Benford, our dedicated copyeditor; to Vicki Gibbs for her copyediting expertise; and to Karen Pecor Hill for her administrative acumen. The love and support we experienced fueled our passion to help women realize the remarkable value of intentional female friendships—for a lifetime!

–Diane and Margaret

Table of Contents

Women I Want to Grow Old With

Introduction

Why This Book Is Designed for You!

Girlfriends. They're our companions, confidants, support groups, play dates, and lifelines. We're at our best when we know they're there for us—leading the way on new adventures or in the background ready to listen when we reach out. They're by our sides in the fun *and* tough times. Through this book, we look at what it takes to be intentional about making and keeping our girlfriends—for a lifetime!

Our friends are as close as sisters, and sometimes they are our sisters! We love to laugh with them and occasionally stir up trouble with 'em! They're our thought partners, voices of reason, and devil's advocates. We double date and search for a mate with them. They let us down and, once in a while, infuriate us. We forgive and so do they. And if we're lucky enough, no matter our age, we'll find women we want to grow old with.

If you have a cadre of women you call your friends, we hope the stories and examples here will help those relationships grow even stronger. If you want to expand your circle of friends or discover new relationships as you turn the pages of your own story, we believe this book will guide and inspire you to do just that. Having trouble with one particular friend? Read how to overcome breakdowns and pitfalls. Find reasons for diversifying your friendships and ways to mix it up when you spend time with friends. Discover ideas for enjoying friends individually and exploring friendship in groups of various sizes and purposes. Even consider committing to becoming a GOTCHA! Group, so you can Grow Old Together with Courage, Health, and Attitude!

Why are we the experts on female friendships? We're not. We're two friends, each who had profound experiences that made her recognize the importance friends have in our journey and to our overall well-being. We spent three years interviewing women about how they build and nurture their circles of friends, and exploring how and why friends contribute so richly to us. We send our gratitude to these special women for sharing their stories. We think they'll inspire you to strengthen your commitment to finding women you want to grow old with as you continue your life journeys.

We hope you enjoy the discovery as much as we did!

Diane and Margaret

P.S. Please visit our website: womeniwanttogrowoldwith.com. Join the conversation on Facebook.com/WomenIWanttoGrowOldWith and on our blog, womeniwanttogrowoldwith.wordpress.com. Follow us on Twitter @GotchaFriends.

Chapter 1

*Do We Have Friends Who Are **Really** There for Us?*

So we think we have plenty of girlfriends? Not so fast. The truth is most of us might be hard-pressed to list the top three women we'd call upon if our lives fell apart today. Most women desperately need female friendships. Yet the urgencies of the moment prevent us from facing this reality. For many reasons, we don't do what we need to do to ensure a rich safety net of women we can rely on when life is good or when all hell breaks loose.

As women we fear being alone or lonely when we move, lose a job, see our kids leave home, suffer the death of a partner or spouse, or even retire. Yet it's easy to brush off that fear with the notion, "Oh, I have friends; I don't need to worry." If we're honest, most of us go on autopilot when it comes to our friends. We don't take deliberate actions to secure our relationships or upgrade our friend-making skills. Can we really afford to be smug or blind to the importance of making and growing our female friendships?

"I have a new-found appreciation for my girlfriends after going through a breakup recently," says Alexis, 25, a personal shopper at a high-end department store. "I mean, where did everyone go while I was spending all my time focusing on being the perfect girlfriend? It's amazing how quickly you notice your lack of effort in your friendships when the romantic relationship is no more. After rounding everyone up again, I saw that anything is possible with the right group of girlfriends. Whom else can we tell our whole lives to, not be judged, and receive comfort from at the same time?

"As women we often feel like it's a luxury to go out with our friends. I say it needs to become a necessity!" Alexis continues. "They are a big part of our sanity, our happiness, and more importantly our hearts. Time is not something that we have, it's something we make—so never become too busy for your girlfriends!"

Whether it's a love relationship, a busy schedule, or just a lack of recognition of the support system they offer that keeps us from attending to our friends, we often experience an inflection point that prompts us to focus on this critical component of our lives.

"I've never been one to have a large number of friends," says Vicki, 62, a freelance writer/editor. "So several years ago, when we moved away from the town I grew up in, I felt lucky to establish two close friendships in my new town. But when my husband began traveling frequently for work, those two friends didn't seem like enough. They both had their own lives and often weren't available when I was. My children are grown, and I work from my home office, so I was alone 24-7. I needed other women to do things with and talk to, so I decided to expand my circle of friends."

At some point, when life crumbles around us, we may experience a sinking feeling that we lack the strong female bonds that would help hold us together. Let's not get caught friendless at the very moment we need friends the most. This book propels us to take action now—and reap the benefits of having women in our lives we want to grow old with. It's so much more satisfying to Grow Old Together with Courage, Health, and Attitude—GOTCHA!

Who Are Our Intention Holders?

We can breathe new life and excitement into our relationships by seeing our female friends as "intention holders"—women who encircle us with their love and support. We feel safe and secure with these women. They are on our sides. They carefully and deliberately hold our goals and dreams. They are the women on speed dial. We call them to celebrate when things go right and for consolation, comfort, and unconditional support when things go wrong. Whether embarking on a new adventure, facing a challenging time, or questioning our ability, we know things will be better if we let these intention holders bring us their goodwill and energy. They can be an army of angels locking their wings around us, providing extra lift to lighten our loads. Literally and figuratively, they are by our sides cheering us on or helping to carry our burdens as we cross yet another finish line.

"Women friends can kick back into your life immediately with no lost time," says Liz, 54, a marketing company senior executive. "You can almost start the conversation with the 'baggage.' You can talk about everything from ailments to depression to being intimate with one special person, all in a single discussion. Sometimes you commiserate, sometimes you celebrate, and sometimes you just accept totally and completely. And, it all makes a huge difference in your love, respect, and appreciation for your long-term friendships."

It's the instant relatedness and unconditional acceptance inherent in female friendships that we appreciate and crave. Women friendships re-create us, inspire us, and bring fulfillment to our lives. They make us feel not so alone. They give us hope. Our best friends can be those whom we may not see for months, even years, yet we're able to reconnect with them with no lost time. They completely *get* us. They unequivocally want us to succeed. As intention holders, they help us get through, get over, and get beyond.

DeeDee, 42, has worked as a journalist and public relations maven for twenty years. She balances a full-time job with two elementary-age children and a husband who is a wonderful support but suffers from depression. Girlfriends are her lifeline.

"My friend Yasmine knows all my history. I can call her any time, and she will support me while also telling me the truth," says DeeDee.

"The other morning before work, my husband had an outburst of anger, and I issued an SOS text message to Yasmine as I got on the commuter train. The minute I got off, we talked, and she listened and echoed back everything I said. I knew she got it.

"Yasmine loves my husband, so she never bashes him. She reassured me and relayed something similar she experienced with her husband. I knew I wasn't alone. As we talked I got an apology e-mail from my husband, and I shared it with her. 'See, he's a good guy,' Yasmine responded. Yasmine's really a good friend. She's there for me and knows what I need when I'm having a tough time with my husband's darkness. She understands that sometimes the solutions she has in mind may not be what I need to hear at the moment. She validates me, allows me to hear myself, and listens to my signals to know if I want advice or if I just need someone to get me. I trust her."

G✷TCHA! MOMENT

When a Friend's in Need, It's Not About You

How can you be a friend in another's moment of crisis and still remain a friend when the crisis passes? Listen to your friend's upset or dilemma with the big picture in mind. When you listen with a mindset of service and support, you are better able to keep your emotions at bay. Remember, the moment is not about you. She may need sound advice but just want a sounding board. If you're listening for what best serves your friendship, you'll know how to respond. Give feedback from a place of love. "However this turns out, I support you, and I'm here for you" shows that you hold the best intention for her.

Friends Are Good for Our Health

The stress caused by busy lifestyles, difficult economic conditions, and aging issues makes the need for female friendships ever present. A strong circle of female friends fills unspeakable voids, provides certainty in an uncertain time, and offers a protective network of love. Research proves that having friends is as important to well-being as paying attention to our health and finances.

- Americans have one-third fewer confidants than we did in the 1980s, according to a Duke University and The University of Arizona study. Twice as many of us say we do not have close friends to share our problems with.

- When women hang out with friends, their bodies release the hormone oxytocin, which combats stress and creates calm, according to a landmark University of California, Los Angeles, study.

- The more friendships women have, the less likely they are to develop physical health issues, and the more easily they recover after the death of a partner, according to the Harvard Medical School Nurses' Health Study.

- Women with friends are twenty-six percent less likely to develop dementia, says a study by Kaiser Permanente, one of the leading health care providers and not-for-profit health plans in the United States, reported in the *American Journal of Public Health.*

Most women spend time investing in their financial futures. If we put that same level of attention into investing in our female friends, we'll protect ourselves in a different but equally powerful way. Even if today our lives are filled with family, work, and pastimes, *tomorrow* may be suddenly different. We must *make* time for friends. Our health depends on it.

Don't Stop Thinking About Tomorrow

This book was born out of need and desire. Both of us, the authors, had deep personal experiences that made us realize how much we wanted and needed girlfriends in our lives, now and in the future.

"When my father died, after sixty years of marriage, my mother literally had no friends left. Although she boldly tried to make friends at age eighty, women in their seventies acted as though she were too old for them, and married women were afraid she'd 'steal' their husbands. Though she had her family, I believe not having friends whom she could share with and lean on added to her overwhelming sense of loneliness and contributed to her passing two years later.

"I also saw my younger sister become a widow at age forty-three. Because my older sister and I lived in different cities, she leaned on a few supportive friends to literally be by her side. The woman who has become her best friend is also a widow. It's not that they focus on their losses, but when my sister brings up a concern—like dreaming about her late husband even though she's happily remarried—her friend eases her fears by letting her know she has had the same experience. It doesn't make it any easier, but my sister doesn't feel so alone. She has someone who completely *gets* her."

—Diane

"Approaching my sixtieth birthday served as a defining moment for me. Thinking about how and with whom I wanted to spend the next decades of my life made me question, 'Do I have any real friends?' and 'What is a real friend?' That, combined with the whole idea of getting older, had me wondering if I would someday be old and friendless. I knew I wanted friends who were committed to being with me, whether I was in the same trench with them or not. I started purposefully asking women I knew and liked to join me for coffee. If, in our conversations, I experienced mutual admiration and connection, I would say, 'Let's be friends,' and ask them point blank, 'Do you want to be one of the women I grow old with?'"

—Margaret

Women need friends *when* they need them—not tomorrow, not next week, but today. We can't just fill that need on demand, like hot water from the tap. We must continually add to our relationship reservoir. But, too often, we don't think about friendship as something to constantly nourish and grow. We just take it for granted. Or we rely on outdated friend-making or friend-keeping skills and habits. We may also be naive, not thinking about what the future might hold. Most women outlive male partners by at least five years, according to sources such as the Harvard University Gazette and WebMD.

Friends literally sustain and protect us. Shouldn't we remove the blinders and address our feelings and behaviors around friendship? Friendship is *within* our control to create and nurture. Being intentional in creating, sustaining, and expanding our friendship circles can safeguard our emotional, physical, and spiritual health. Remember, we have a say in the matter.

G✳TCHA! MOMENT

Create a Blueprint of Your Circle of Friends

Imagine your friendships as a circle of support, helping you not be or feel alone as you move through life. Take a moment to create a visual representation of your current circle of friends. It's OK if the circle is small or unpopulated for now. This powerful tool will get you in touch with the reality of your existing friendships. It will also support you in expanding your friendship circle.

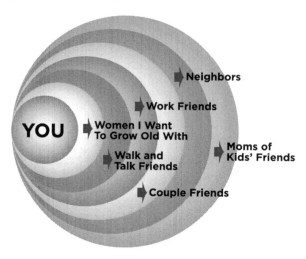

* Imagine yourself in the middle of concentric circles. See your closest friends in the innermost circle next to you. These are your most intimate friends with whom you can share your deepest fears, concerns, and joys. You can turn to them *at any time*.

* Place your other friends and acquaintances in the re-maining circles based on what roles they play in your life. You might name your circles: Intention Holders, Ex-ercise Friends, Work Friends, Book Club Friends, Parents of Kids' Friends, Vacation Friends, and New Friends. A woman may be in more than one circle. Perhaps New Friends is your outermost circle.

* Have fun with this concept. Put your friends' names on sticky notes (so you can move them later if you want to), and place them in the appropriate circle.

Or cut out paper dolls and name them, use snapshots of your gal pals, or find pictures of women in magazines that resemble your friends, and arrange them in the circles. A circle mobile or collage can be fun too. Design your circle on an electronic tablet or social media site. Be creative with whatever expression excites you most. Designing a physical representation of your existing circle of friends allows you to see what support system you have in place today. With this clearer picture, you may now see areas in which you might want to strengthen your safety net.

* Evaluate the amount of energy and time you're spending with the friends in each circle. Ask yourself: "Are there any changes I want to make? Any shifts in where I spend my time? Anyone I'd like to draw into my inner circle who's not already there?"

* Take a hard look at any friendships that may have become exhausting, difficult, or draining. Decide how you want to manage these relationships to free up time and energy for more fulfilling and rewarding ones.

* We'll come back to this concept throughout the book, so keep your Friendship Circle at the ready! Our goal is to help you create a close circle of friends inside of which you will Grow Old Together with Courage, Health, and Attitude—GOTCHA! Throughout the book, we'll provide examples of women who are doing just that.

Don't Wake Up Fifty and Friendless

If having a close circle of female friends is so important, how can we wake up one day and find ourselves fifty and feeling friendless? We might say, "Not me, I have lots of friends!" But let's take stock. Whom do we reach out to when we feel emotionally alone? Whom do we turn to when confronting an illness, depression, financial fears, or the belief that we've done the unforgivable? Is our safety net of friends strong and deep enough to truly be there for us? Do we have women who are holding good intentions for our fulfillment and happiness?

A few years ago, Margaret began her journey to discover and acquire female friendships at a whole new level. Being a friendly person, Margaret had lots of people in her life, but she began to question the loyalty and depth of those friendships. Margaret felt alone. She saw that many of her relationships were project oriented and results focused—volunteering, raising money for causes, growing a successful business, and, sometimes, even being a wife and mother. With her busy schedule, she and her friends would often *catch up* with each other's lives but not necessarily be an ongoing *part* of each other's lives. Margaret began to realize that she wanted women in her life who were willing to "committedly" share their lives in a broad and satisfying way. She purposefully asked those women with whom she felt a connection to join her for coffee, lunch, or a walk. As mentioned before, at some point, she'd boldly ask, "Do you want to be one of the women I grow old with?" Happily, these special women wanted the same thing. In fact, the idea resonated—"I love it!" "I need that!" and "I want to grow old with you, too!"

Friendships aren't something we can leave to chance. We can't wish friends into existence; we can only create them through our time, goodwill, and energy. Let's get real about whether or not we have an authentic intention to develop and sustain friendships in our lives. If we don't pay attention to this area of our life now, can we guarantee we'll have the friends we want when we need them the most?

As savvy women today, we know that if we have a male partner—unless he's many years younger—chances are he's going to die before we do. We don't have to look far to imagine ourselves alone. Consciously or unconsciously, statistics about women living longer than men heighten our fears. We worry about what will happen if our partner passes away or our love relationship dissolves. Some women are weary with being "married singles" and feel alone or lonely even with a spouse.

At any age we may not realize that our lives are void of the joy and fulfillment close friends can bring, until it suddenly hits us in the heart. Six years ago, Allison, 38, vice president of recruiting for an ad agency, had a "ton of friends." But with a busy job, dating, volunteer work, and deciding to let go of a few relationships because of differing values, her friendships dwindled.

"I love my mother, but there are certain things you don't ask your mother—things you can only ask your best friend," says Allison. "I have a lot of women in my life, but I no longer have one friend I can call up and tell everything. Occasionally, I'll go out to dinner with someone I meet at a philanthropic event, and we become best friends for a night. But there's no contact after that. That's exactly why I don't have a close friend to turn to for advice or to ask basic questions. I watch television and see women going out with their best friends, and I say, 'Really, huh?' I long to have someone super close."

Allison says that she recently went to a luncheon and met twenty fabulous women, but she didn't try to get to know any of them more personally or suggest getting together at another time.

"You have to be bold to risk talking to someone new to see if there's compatibility," she continues. "I'm not risk adverse in my career, financial planning, or looking for the right guy. But, when it comes to connecting with new girlfriends, I stop short. I tell myself I don't have time to be the kind of friend I want to be, and I don't want to short-change them. It's also tough to know what I want in a friend and what I can bring to her in return. Yet, at the same time, I feel disadvantaged because I don't have a bond with one or two special women. I actually am in deep thought about this; I think about it every day. I want things to change."

Allison is a "make-what-I-want-happen" kind of person. She pays close attention to orchestrating the important parts of her life. Taking a moment to think about her friendships gave her pause. The realization that she didn't have the close friends she wanted prompted her to consider taking concerted action in pursuing friendships. Just as we take responsibility for our educations, careers, and finances to deal with the unpredictability of life, it makes sense to prepare for our futures by generating strong circles of friends.

Marie, 50, an executive, says it's easy for her to have superficial talk at an event or function, but it takes energy to go a little further. "If I've exchanged business cards with a woman with whom I feel a certain connection, I listen to my intuition and follow up in two to three days with an e-mail or a call to set up breakfast or lunch," she says. "When we meet, I focus on what we have in common and our core values and then build on that foundation. It's incredible because just a little effort opens up new and deeper relationships, not just with that one individual but often with other women I know. Suddenly, I've expanded my friendship circle."

We're not alone in the world, and so we don't have to settle for being alone. A world of girlfriends awaits us. If we really want them, we will find them—and they'll find us. It may take stepping out in a new direction, risking a little pride, or shaking up our routine and trying something new, but we *can* uncover these precious jewels we call friends.

G✻TCHA! MOMENT

How Not to Let a Would-Be Friend Slip Away

When you've interacted with a woman you think you could be friends with, try this simple process we call ASK:

1. **Acknowledge** the interest you have in exploring a friendship and the connection you feel. "It was such

a pleasure getting to know someone who shares my passion for good movies (helping younger women or cooking with organic foods)."

2. **Seek out** the next opportunity to connect. "It was so much fun talking with you. Let's exchange e-mail addresses and set up another time to meet."

3. **Keep your commitment** to contact her and your determination to explore a possible friendship.

Is Fear Standing in Our Way?

So what stops us from reaching out to new women we meet? What keeps us from following up with an e-mail or a call?

Simply said, it's fear: fear that we don't have the time, fear that we won't relate or be accepted, fear that we'll feel denied or betrayed, or fear of failing at something we think should be second nature. Or it may be that we're afraid that this new friend won't fit into our current circle of friends. Perhaps secretly we wonder if she's too pretty, too poised, too financially sound, too educated, too young, too old, too funny, too sad, too lonely, "too, too, too" for us or that we are "too, too, too" for her. This kind of "too, too, too" talk keeps us from taking committed actions that will result in lasting, satisfying friendships.

As we researched this book, we heard repeatedly that, as women, we want real friends, the kind who accept and nourish one another—not just Facebook friends or one hundred forty-character Twitter followers, but face-to-face and heart-to-heart friends with whom we can laugh and cry and just get real. We want to be able to reach down under where the pain is to a place that cements, bonds, and seals the connection. Virtual interactions help, but face time is what matters most. Girlfriends give important dimension to our lives. If we ignore this vital facet, we could be subject to a sudden and rude awakening.

Pat, 64, a business development consultant, says that girlfriends have always been a vital part of her life. However, when she was traveling a lot for business, she let her friendships slip away.

"When I traveled 150,000 miles a year, worked eighty hours a week, and barely had time to go to the cleaners to get my clothes, I *lost* my network of friends," says Pat, married thirty years, with a son and daughter. "It's the worst thing I ever did. When my job ended, I didn't know whom to call. I felt so alone. I'd think, 'Maybe I should call so and so,' and then I'd realize I hadn't talked to her for a few years. Or I'd remember another friend who had called me a while ago, but I didn't make time to return her call. I swallowed my pride, got really busy reaching out, and made lots of apologies. Honesty was the only way to go. I told them how much I'd been traveling, that I rarely slept at home three nights in a row, and how sorry I was for not keeping in touch. Eventually I built up and even expanded my network of female friends. I vowed never to let that happen again. It was painful and embarrassing. There is more to life than work; I had lost all sense of balance.

"Now I believe that if you let go of your friendships, it's one-sided and just about you," continues Pat. "If you maintain them, it's about you *and* your friends with lots of give and take. Once I started getting back in touch, I realized how much I had missed visiting with my friends in person or on the phone. Life is so much better and fuller with my girlfriends. There's honesty between girlfriends you can't have otherwise. You can't call up your kids and tell them all that you're dealing with; they aren't the audience to lay that on."

Looking back, Pat sees how her girlfriends have been there for all the major transitions of her life, such as when her husband lost his job. Suddenly she was the major breadwinner.

"I needed a support system because I wasn't used to the pressure. I couldn't complain to my spouse and make him feel worse. My friends allowed me to release the anger and get beyond it. And hearing from other women whose partners weren't making financial contributions put me at ease."

When a skiing accident temporarily paralyzed her son, Pat once again experienced the value of her family and friends.

"I wouldn't have gotten through that without my girlfriends," she says. "The trauma was so great and so deep that I just didn't know what to do. My friends stepped in and connected with me at a very special level. Today I'm more conscious about making an effort to reach out to the women in my life."

In life, we have what we are committed to, and we have what is urgent. Often what's urgent usurps and displaces what we are committed to. Make time today to cultivate tomorrow's friendships.

It's critical to look at female friendship through a different lens and confront the unexamined thinking that allows circumstances to control our lives. Let's not be lulled into believing we've got "that friendship thing" handled, like a frog unaware of impending boiling water. We can't be numb to the consequences of today's choices. We can create a circle of friends now to support and protect us for a lifetime. A future of friendships by design!

Chapter 2

Debunking Friend-Making Myths:
Time to Brush Up on Our Skills?

Many women say it's not that easy to make new friends. It takes a certain amount of personal risk to initiate a relationship—especially when everyone's life *seems* so busy. Let's accept the fact that not everyone we reach out to will reciprocate, and not take it personally. But when a new potential friend does respond, let's seize the moment!

"You just can't over-estimate the glory of a budding friendship. I'm as giddy as a school girl with a crush whenever my new friend calls," says Alexandra, 40, who leads a technology and consulting company. "There's such a soul-filling goodness associated with a woman friend…and it's so needed in what can be a soul-sucking reality for women trying to be and do it all."

So how do we move from a whiny, "It's so hard to meet new women" point of view to a confident, "I know I will make new friends" mindset? First and foremost, let's be open to new possibilities.

Friendship Myths and Excuses

Let's ask ourselves if we've bought into any of these friendship myths and excuses that derail us from our intentions:

- A *best* friend can only be someone I've known since childhood and who has an intimate accounting of my past.
- I'm just too busy to find new friends—one or two good friends are all I need.

- Every woman has her circle of friends; I'm not outgoing enough to break in.
- Keeping in touch with friends online is enough social contact for me.
- I'm not good enough, smart enough, or worldly enough to be her friend.
- I've got enough friends in my neighborhood…on the volunteer committee, at church, in my book club, etc.
- I only want friends who are like me.
- Most of the people I know are from work; I can't mix business and pleasure.

Many of us have perpetuated these myths and excuses for years. This thinking inhibits us from making new friendships. It may even allow existing friends to slip away or become mediocre at best.

G✳TCHA! MOMENT

Open Your Mind to New Thinking

Open your mind to new thinking by answering these questions:

- ✳ What gets in my way of connecting with other women?
- ✳ What messages, spoken or unspoken, do I send to others?
- ✳ Am I open to women with certain personalities and tastes?
- ✳ Do I think good friends are only women I've known for years?
- ✳ What qualities do I bring to the relationship?

❋ Can I courageously break the ice when I meet a woman who could be a friend?

Unexamined Beliefs Limit Our Friendships

When we let preconceived notions and a few bad experiences about friendship go unexamined and unchallenged, we limit ourselves to the same old way of thinking and behaving. But if we step back and consider new possibilities, we can embrace an exciting future.

Take a moment to look at how our negative thinking can perpetuate a faulty belief system. Often our existing points of view thwart the desired outcome of expanding our circle of friends. Notice how this is illustrated in Margaret's stories below.

Negative Thought: I'm not outgoing enough to meet new friends.

Faulty Belief: My friendship quotient is a *fait accompli*. I'll never have the number of friends I want.

Unwanted Outcome: We live inside a limiting assumption and settle for one or two friends. We even stop looking for, or being open to, ways of attracting more women.

Years ago, Margaret remembers suggesting to her sister Barbara that she have more than one friend. At the time, Barbara was happy with having just one intimate friend. But just questioning her belief that a single best friend was fine started Barbara thinking and behaving differently. Today she has many friends—and many call her their "best" friend.

Negative Thought: I can't build a strong and intimate relationship with someone new.

Faulty Belief: Only someone who's known me for a long time can *really* be my friend.

Inevitable Outcome: We don't allow new relationships to take root and mature.

Margaret has always envied women who have friends they've known since childhood. Her tumultuous early life and many moves didn't allow for that to happen. She felt she had missed opportunities for those kinds of deep, satisfying friendships.

Holding onto a belief system we've had since we were young can keep this way of thinking in place. But does a friend have to be someone who knew our high school sweetheart, attended our wedding, or was at our side when we turned single…again? Can't a new friend quickly get to know how our past has shaped us?

Margaret realized that she could create meaningful friendships at any time in her life. While her new friend may not know all her prior victories and defeats, she *can* know who Margaret is today and become part of her tomorrows.

Negative Thought: I don't have *enough* in common with her to be friends.

Faulty Belief: To be friends with someone, we should have fairly similar backgrounds, interests, family composition, careers, etc.

Inevitable Outcome: This limited belief boxes us in and prevents us from opening our lives to the many wonderful women around us. Another's diverse interests and experiences can open our eyes and our worlds.

As a new member of a foundation that supports significant philanthropy, Margaret didn't feel the other women in the group could ever be more than committee colleagues. After one meeting she mentioned to another member that she didn't think she was of the same "ilk" as the other foundation members.

"What?" the member exclaimed. "You're an interesting woman with a great background and such a positive outlook; I'm sure any of these women would value your friendship."

With that fresh perspective, Margaret questioned her former assumptions and took action to squash the myth. She began inviting women to coffee just to get to know them better. Asking questions about their passions and careers fostered interesting and intimate discoveries about each other.

Negative Thought: My friend isn't putting as much energy into the relationship. She's not reciprocating; I'm going to end the relationship.

Faulty Belief: We must keep score and both contribute equally at all times.

Inevitable Outcome: We see the relationship as just one more failed attempt. We lump it into the pile of "casual" friendships, and the relationship peters out.

In her friendship exploration, Margaret's internal chatter supported the faulty belief that because the other person hadn't called or invited her to a function, it meant the woman didn't care about her or wasn't interested in a friendship. At first this made her upset, and she wanted to pull away. As a leadership coach, Margaret knew enough to realize she had a faulty belief at play. She feared loss, being alone, and feeling unwanted. Seeing this allowed her to reconnect to her desire to cultivate friendships, and she became more willing to pick up the phone or send an e-mail. When she did, the friend typically reacted positively, adding one more strong thread to the friendship fabric.

What negative thoughts and beliefs can we release to actualize a future of limitless friendship opportunities? Taking time to analyze our thoughts and beliefs enables us to shift our thinking to achieve better, more fulfilling outcomes. Rationalizing that we'll do it later, when life is a little more settled, is a sucker's bet. Be careful! When our lives are completely settled, it usually means we're dead! Now is the time to intentionally build our circle of women we want to grow old with.

Feeling Friendless? We're Not Alone

There are many reasons we grow tired of not having enough female companionship in our lives. A huge void may result after the loss of a partner, sister, or dear friend. We may move away from friends and lose their closeness. Often it's the busyness of life that prevents us from connecting and staying connected with women, even though we want and need them in our lives.

"I work alone out of a home office, and I fear isolation because it takes a lot of effort to reach out to others. I'm not sure I have the energy or the time it takes to develop relationships right now," says Julie, 46, a public relations practitioner. "My life with my husband and two daughters is very fulfilling, yet I know I am missing something. Having a couple of closer friends would complete my life, but it often feels overwhelming to think about the work those relationships would require. I have a friend who calls me up to let me know she'll be in town in three to four weeks. While I want to see her, I have difficulty planning so far ahead like that…my life seems all about the kids right now, and so I'm not able to see her as much as I'd like."

If we're not mindful of our rationale and excuses, we can create a self-fulfilling prophecy of friendship scarcity versus abundance. Research shows that loneliness causes stress, which increases the risk of cardiovascular disease and immune system disorders. It can lead to feelings of depression, which decrease a woman's motivation to establish a solid support group that will be there no matter what.

As a result of her husband's work transfers, Pat, 64, moved eight times in twelve years.

"Relocating forced me to be adaptable and learn to make friends," she says. "I could sit inside and sulk, which I occasionally did, or risk opening up myself and my home and meet new people. I invited neighbors I'd never met to Super Bowl parties, Fourth of July barbecues, and progressive dinners. Sometimes lots of people showed up; sometimes only a few. I often wondered, 'Why me? Why do I always have to be the initiative taker?' But I always met some really wonderful people.

"Occasionally someone reached out to me," continues Pat. "I moved to Atlanta nine months pregnant on a hot Labor Day weekend. Unable to bend over with a three-year-old running around me, I still tried to unpack the dishes. A wonderful neighbor I hadn't yet met came by with iced tea. We became immediate friends. Her gesture gave me hope that everything would be OK and reinforced that reaching out to other women is well worth the effort."

Like all other worthwhile adventures, making friends takes time, passion, and commitment, but the rewards are huge!

Be Deliberate: Friends Don't "Just Happen"

When we feel our social networks have unraveled for one reason or another and a sense of isolation is taking hold, that's the moment we need to do more, not less, to bring new friends into our lives. Being stuck in our circumstances will only perpetuate what we most fear: loneliness.

Recently someone suggested Margaret contact friends from her "old neighborhood" and set up a gathering. Margaret thought about calling some of those people, but the distance that had developed through lack of communication over the years made the telephone seem like it weighed ten thousand pounds. A sense of failure took hold, making her doubt her ability to create lasting friendships. Instead of retreating, however, Margaret decided to learn from her past. She reconnected with the mother of one of her daughter's friends. They met for dinner and are now exploring their relationship on a whole new level.

It doesn't matter what age or stage of life we're at—the need for girl-friends is ever present. After losing her husband of sixty years, Diane's eighty-year-old mother, Charlotte, moved from California to Oregon to be near her daughter. She found it difficult to insert herself into the lives of the women she met. But she forced herself to volunteer, which led to an invitation to a book club. Dragging herself to the local health club, she saw women showing up early for coffee and followed suit. On daily walks, she stopped neighbors and introduced herself. She even asked one woman, who had recently lost her husband, "Are you lonely?" Surprised by the straight question, the woman answered, "Yes," and the two got together for tea. They became good friends.

Bold? Yes. Gutsy? Yes. But if we take risks, if we get out of our comfort zones and be vulnerable, it's worth the effort.

Diane's husband began traveling extensively when they moved from San Diego to Oakland, California. She knew she'd feel more connected if she found a church. The first Sunday at one small church, several women reached out to her after the service and invited her to stay for coffee. She asked for their phone numbers and kept in touch. Over time, Diane developed three close friendships, and today their interests go well beyond their faith and values. When she needed new friends the most, Diane pushed herself out the door and did the uncomfortable.

It's easy to say to ourselves, "I couldn't do that! I'm not that kind of person"; "I can't ask someone to be my friend or ask for her phone number"; or "Yes, I admire those traits, but that's not me." If we consider for a moment that we really *are* that kind of person, we might be open to the possibility that somewhere along life's journey we decided to be careful about whom we reach out to. We may have told ourselves that we were too shy to initiate a conversation or too proud to just up and ask someone to be our friend. Maybe subconsciously we believe we don't deserve the friends we really want. In those myths, lies, and excuses, we withdraw and withhold ourselves from others. Yet, all the while, we really want to be that daring, confident woman who goes for what she wants and gets it.

Beginning a Friendship—The First Step

Who hasn't joined an existing group—be it a new job, bridge group, sports league, professional organization, etc.—and gotten a sinking feeling that we didn't fit in? It's no fun feeling like everyone is on the inside, but we're on the outside. It's awful wondering when or if we'll ever connect in an intimate way.

How do we take that first step to initiate a conversation and not fool ourselves into thinking, "If she wants to be my friend, she'll let me know"? How do we not let the moment slip by?

"I often see something in a woman that has the right chemistry for a friendship, and then I get stopped," says Lynn, 57, a nurse and chief experience officer for a health system. "Someone has to take the first step, but I hold back because I feel constrained by time. I want to get over that."

Some women are introverted, which keeps them from reaching out. Often they're grateful that other women have the guts to speak up first. If we're willing to take that risk, we may find others appreciate our effort.

Maybe we're not shy, but we've bought into the lie that the other person couldn't be interested in *us*. Indulging in self-deprecating beliefs keeps us from taking new action. Without changing our internal dialogue, we'll stay in a rut. Growth is uncomfortable. We can't get to a new branch until we let go of another. We create new possibilities in our lives when we shift our thinking. Admit it! We're worthy of new friends. We *do* have the sense of humor, life experience, perspective, compassion, love, etc. to bring value to relationships. With this stance, our actions will change.

G✳TCHA! MOMENT

Excuses Squash Friendship Opportunities

Don't lose the chance to pursue a new friendship with an excuse like "I don't have time" or "This is just a moment for pleasantries; nothing will come from this." Think instead "Now could be a defining moment for a new and vital friendship," and then, more importantly, take action. Here are six quick steps to make a connection in the moment and begin a new friendship.

✳ Dismiss the excuses that flood your head and hold you back, such as "I don't have time for one more relationship in my life," "She doesn't seem interested," or "We may not have enough in common."

✳ Look receptive and interested. Smile—and with your eyes too!

✳ Break the silence with a relevant comment, or ask an engaging question.

✳ Look for a point of connection or commonality, and use it to move the conversation forward.

✳ Wrap up the new connection by exchanging e-mail addresses and phone numbers to keep in touch.

✳ Remember to follow up and follow through, even if some time passes. These are critical next steps in building new friendships.

But What Do We Say to Start a Conversation?

Even when we do strike up a conversation, sometimes the right words don't come to mind. We can get tongue-tied when we censor ourselves and judge our thoughts. Our words don't have to be poetry. We're just opening the door of possibility.

When breaking the ice, look for things to connect to or comment on. It may be a book she's reading, a child's smile, or her taste in shoes. Often, the simplest of things can create an instant bond.

Our journey to write this book began just like that. Margaret was leading a breakout session at a women's leadership conference that Diane was attending. At lunch the topic of "sons" came up, and with just a few comments about our experiences as mothers with adolescent sons, a whole new arena of relatedness opened up. This led to a scheduled coffee date, and, as they say, "the rest is history."

"There's something about our womanhood that allows women to connect if we just express what we're thinking or feeling," says Donna, 67, a retired health-care executive—now a consultant—who grows avocados and coffee on the island of Hawaii. "I couldn't walk into a room of men and say, 'Oh, I love that piece of jewelry,' but I can with a woman. We can help each other have a conversation by connecting to our feminine side."

On a plane ride from San Francisco to Atlanta, Diane asked the woman next to her the simple question, "Are you from the Bay Area?" Within minutes of sharing backgrounds, Diane realized that Mimi's husband was the executive recruiter who helped her land a job more than a dozen years ago. They also discovered that they lived just a few miles apart and went to the same manicurist! The two women exchanged business cards and decided to meet for a walk. When they did, the points of confluence amazed them. This friendship treasure now exists because each took the risk to get to know one another.

Rejection Isn't Personal

Sometimes we've got to be willing to let go when we extend a hand of friendship, and the gesture is not returned. Margaret met a woman, we'll call her Sam, who shared some of her interests, and she followed up in an effort to get to know her better. Initially Sam's enthusiasm for the friendship was strong, but after a few months, the relationship seemed strained. Finally Margaret asked her new friend if she wanted to continue pursuing their friendship. Sam responded with a candid and forthright "no."

While shocked by the response, Margaret graciously let her know if circumstances changed, she'd still like to get to know her better. It took a few days to process what had occurred. Margaret could interpret it as "Nobody loves me, everybody hates me..." or as "She and I just weren't on the same page when it came to pursuing friendship at that particular moment." By choosing the latter, Margaret allowed herself to let go of any "meaning," move on, and be available to start anew with other women.

What's Our Connection Disconnect?

Sometimes, we shut women out of our lives before giving them a chance. It's easy to label others and compare: "She's married; I'm not." "She has children; I don't." "She doesn't work; I do." "She runs marathons; I couldn't crawl a 1K."

Judging brings with it assumptions and often false ones. Limiting whom we count as friends makes our circle of possibilities smaller and smaller. It takes the fun out of discovering new ways to expand our friendship universes—and fresh ways of experiencing the world.

After relocating for a job, Kate, 52, started attending a local church and signed up for kitchen duty. There, with women who had known each other for years, she volunteered to do anything. Among the pots and pans, these women got to "see" Kate as a wife, grandmother, and hardworking professional, not the Kate they may have "imagined" when the tall, stylish woman walked into the chapel alone.

If we're open to exploring friendship and allowing room for diversity and uncertainty, surprising and delightful miracles can result.

Jacqueline, 62, an information technology consultant, said that until eight years ago, she felt disconnected from her girlfriends because they seemed to be growing in different directions. When she enrolled in a leadership retreat, the women there depended on one another as they kayaked, hiked, and river rafted. With this experience, she fully understood the value other women could bring her.

"At work, where I meet most people I know, there's not a lot of rallying for each other, just brute force," says Jacqueline, who works in a male-dominated profession. "Once I saw what supportive women bring to the party, I suddenly started meeting women I *do* want to grow old with. I realize that friendship is about you valuing others and them valuing you—and demonstrating that to each other. It's a completely different relationship than I'm used to, and I want more of that."

Like Jacqueline, our points of view have everything to do with the willingness to attract and even keep friends. By changing our thinking, a different outcome can result. We attract what we want, so let's be clear about what we *do* want!

What Qualities Do We Bring to the Friendship?

It's common to size up our friends by what they bring to our lives. But do we think about what *we* add to the relationships? What's *our* contribution? How do we respond when a friend calls to celebrate good news, ask an opinion, or complain? Do we create a safe place where she can talk about almost anything and be real?

Are we vulnerable ourselves? If our friend shares openly, but we clam up and never delve below the surface, it will soon seem like a one-way street. She may begin to shut down around us and choose someone else with whom she can be candid and transparent.

In her consulting career, Margaret has coached individuals on how to have open and honest communication. She knows that both parties must have a commitment to the relationship. If one friend is willing to risk not appearing perfect but the other is not, the relationship is on slippery ground. Intimacy draws friends closer.

G✸TCHA! MOMENT

To Have a Friend, You Must Be a Friend

Take time to evaluate how you *show up* in your friendships. Here's a ten-point checklist. Do you:
1. Listen well and ask questions to learn more?
2. Explore with interest her likes, dislikes, passions, and disappointments?
3. Appropriately challenge her thinking?
4. Speak the truth in kindness?
5. Keep your commitments?
6. Ask for feedback, ideas, and opinions?
7. Serve as a good sounding board?
8. Encourage?
9. Provide a sense of connection?
10. Brainstorm and dream together?

In other words, do you allow your friend to feel nurtured and supported? Do you let her give the same to you?

Making Time for Friends

One of the biggest barriers that gets in the way of creating new friends, or growing existing ones, is the decision that we don't have the time. It feels like being with friends will detract from the *rest* of our lives. In reality, connecting with friends increases our sense of vitality, motivation, and purpose.

As a pediatric ICU nurse who works the night shift and is attending school full time to get a double master's degree, Amanda, 26, carefully makes time for her friends.

"I'm often sleeping when others are awake or have a day off. If I work Friday nights, my Saturdays are cut short from catching up on my sleep," says Amanda. "I have to plan in advance to see my friends and be very organized; I'm not spontaneous right now. But my close girlfriends are important to me because they offer me the ability to talk about personal problems, desires, and plans. I don't feel like I have to work to impress them; they know exactly who I am. Plus I need them to goof off with!"

Amanda looks at her work and school schedules to build in time to travel the hour and a half from Tampa to Ocala, Florida, to see her good friend Laura-Ashley. She calls weeks ahead to make tentative plans and then confirms a few days out, since Laura-Ashley doesn't like to plan too far in advance.

"We typically go out for a meal with our friend Silvana and then go back to her place to drink wine, play video games, eat sushi, and just catch up," says Amanda. "I often spend the night since Jimmy, her husband, is a worship leader and works a lot of late hours. When he comes home, he just gives us our space, so we have plenty of girl time."

If we've neglected our friendships because we think we just can't fit in one more thing, it's time to make plans to reconnect. A lot of friendships can be reclaimed if we're just willing to take simple actions, such as:

- Writing a note, text, or e-mail apologizing for our lack of attention.
- Sending a private message on Facebook expressing our desire to reconnect.
- Leaving a voice mail with a best time of day to call back.
- Suggesting a time and date to get together.

Once we have a concrete plan to rendezvous, it's essential that we stick to our commitment. Time spent with friends to unwind, unload, and reenergize is a valued and critical component of our lives.

Making Friends Can Be a Lifelong Adventure

Sometimes we feel that our current number of friends is sufficient. We think we don't need any more people in our lives. But if our bank accounts had a healthy balance and we got word that more money was available to us, would we turn it down? If we could have more love, would we want it? If we could have an unlimited number of *satisfying* friendships, would we go for it?

Friends move in and out of our lives. Even if today we have a strong team of friends, it's still important to build bench strength—to continually add to our solid support group of friends who will be there for us no matter what.

Lynn, 57, has been married for thirty-five years and has two adult daughters. Even though she has many friends, she knows the importance of making new ones.

"I'm always interested in adding wonderful people to my life," she says. "It's a woman's energy that draws me to a possible new friend. I'll see a woman who is animated and think, 'Oh, I could be friends with her.' But what makes me stay friends with that woman is when I feel safe to be myself and to know that my conversation will go nowhere else. I am looking for a woman who will be frank and say, 'You may want to rethink that; I think you may be wrong.' I like someone who can level with me, but in a helping way. I have a good friend of thirty years, and she has a great way of just picking up the phone to say, 'I was just thinking about you and wanted to check in to know that everything is OK.' Now, that's a friend."

Good friends allow us to hear ourselves speak and bring deep-seated issues to the surface. The friends who let us "find ourselves" usually become close friends—sometimes best friends. They're our therapists and gurus, soul mates, and confidants.

On a daily morning call, Tamara, 60, a nurse practitioner, and Valerie, 45, an occupational therapist, create their day. They talk about what they're doing and determine what outcomes they want to achieve during the next twenty-four hours. What accountability partners!

Diane talks by phone to her sister Karen almost every weekday morning while driving to work. In these precious ten minutes, they update each other, rant and rave, get "expert" counsel, and make sure they hear each other's voice. The ritual is a stabilizing force in their lives and provides daily connection even though they live in different states.

Diane and Leslie, friends since fifth grade, are amazed by their enduring forty-five-plus years of friendship. When something goes wrong, Leslie immediately speed-dials Diane. One harrowing day Leslie counted down to 5:00 p.m. to call Diane. Diane was in her car and caught the desperate phone call live. Seeking solace and understanding, Leslie confided in Diane, knowing it would go no further.

It's great knowing that someone cares about the details of our lives, from the small everyday trials to the major accomplishments. This sense of connectedness is not something we can buy—it only comes from investing in our friends.

Chapter 3

What a Friend Is and Isn't!

- Have we carefully thought about the attributes we want in a friend?
- What are we willing and unwilling to tolerate?
- Are we being the kind of friend we want to have?
- Who are the women we let into our inner circle?
- Are we focusing on women who are interested in a *real* friendship?

Most of us want to have friends and be a friend. But what does that mean? To get clear, let's start by articulating what we expect *from* our friends and what we hold ourselves accountable for *as* a friend. Knowing what we're willing and able to compromise on in a friendship and what would be a complete "deal breaker," causing us to terminate a relationship, is critical. By sorting out our own feelings and priorities, we're able to take a stand for the friendships we have and the friends we want to grow old with.

"I want my friends to feel free to be however they are with me and for them to know that works because I want to be the same with them," says Donna, 52, a hairstylist. "Intimacy is important too. I want deep and real connections, not just a superficial accounting of their lives. I can get that from the supermarket checkout clerk."

As we interviewed women about what a friend is and is *not*, common themes emerged. We came away with seven key *friendship attributes* necessary to develop and strengthen winning relationships. Learning how other women characterize true friendship helps evaluate our own relationships. It causes us to stop and think clearly about what we personally value in our friends and where to put our time, energy, and attention.

"A friend is someone who will share in our good times and our bad times. She has empathy and offers good advice," says Lynn, 55, a Washington, D.C., health-care attorney. "She's a good listener, not just a good talker. She's someone I can call with no hesitation when something positive happens. Regardless of what's going on in her life, she can compartmentalize and be happy for me. She doesn't pretend her own issues don't exist. Being a friend means being able to be honest and transparent and to articulate our feelings inside the friendship. As friends, we're not afraid to share who we really are and what we're really going through."

"I'm looking for safety in conversation, whether enjoying the spa, sipping a glass of wine, or walking on the beach," says Donna, 67. "I want a friend who respects what I say and will not take what I say and do something with it."

Adds Dodi, 51, a workforce health and wellness expert, "What makes a really good friend is someone who is versatile. That means we can talk about 'important' issues like whether to wear a French or color manicure, go shopping and muse about Spanx, or connect on a deeper emotional level on topics such as how to deal with an aging parent."

Deb, 50, a coach, consultant, and single mother of two beautiful daughters, calls her friends witnesses of her life. "One of the things I love about my friend Julie is that she's one of my biggest fans," says Deb. "Whenever I talk to Julie, she is interested in what I am doing and genuinely thrilled by my progress. She openly shares her wins and challenges with me so I can show up as the kind of friend I want to be. I've collected friends over the years, but I cultivate and prune them as I grow. I'm intentional about who I have in my life. I want women with whom I connect at a certain level—a sister of my heart. To me, a friend whom I can call any time and go deep with, who will be there to support me and allow me to support her is a treasure—a gift I give myself."

These women's feelings capture the essence of the following top seven friendship attributes that help determine what a friend is and isn't.

FUN:
Laughter Bonds

ACCOUNTABILITY:
Holding Each Other
Responsible to Our Values

TRANSPARENCY &
AUTHENTICITY: Being
Who You Say You Are

RECIPROCATION:
The Responsibility
to Give Back

LISTENING:
So Others Can
Be Heard

TRUST:
Building on Solid
Foundation

LOYALTY: Being
There for One
Another

Trust: Building on a Solid Foundation

Trust is not only foundational to relationships but a friendship characteristic that women value highly. Most women love sharing their feelings with the intimacy and openness that it brings. To consider a relationship "safe," trust must be present. Without it, the relationship remains shallow and superficial. It isn't necessary to have shared a history with lots of common interests or hang out regularly to enjoy an intimate, open, and trust-filled relationship. Fostering and nurturing trust forms timeless bonds.

Throughout her life, Margaret has enjoyed the rich blessings that come from supporting causes that make a difference, be it a school board, fundraiser, or philanthropic organization. She felt confident in her friendships with the women in these groups who shared her vision and even rallied in the trenches with her to make their joint vision a reality. Several years ago, with a change in a particular board of directors, Margaret suddenly found herself "outside" the leadership group that she worked so diligently in for many years. The experience was quite upsetting to her. She felt separate and alone, even though she continued to support the cause as a member.

Margaret began to question whom she could trust and who would *really* stand for her as a friend. Once her trust eroded, the foundation for friendship did as well. Margaret now sees that she had an unspoken assumption that the women in the leadership group were there for *each other* as well as for the cause. She now differentiates "associates" from true friends. She realizes that trust in friendship includes *articulating* a commitment to friends—to be there for each other and to have each other's back. Today Margaret will openly express that commitment in an effort to build the trust she desires in her friendships.

We've probably all experienced the pain that results from misplaced trust. It's no fun to feel the sting of betrayal. We can usually recount the exact time, place, and circumstances when a friendship faltered around trust issues.

So how do we earn and keep our friend's trust? It's as basic as making commitments and sticking to them, and as simple as believing that our friend is acting with our best interests in mind. Trust is sacred, and like a savings account, it builds over time. We can make occasional small withdrawals and still have a strong balance, but a major withdrawal will wipe out the account. For example, we may accept a momentary slip of the tongue. But when a friend to whom we've entrusted intimate details uses those details against us, trust breaks down in a major way. And once it's completely broken, regaining trust usually requires a long, arduous journey of ongoing proof that we can be trusted again—a journey many are unwilling to take.

When trust starts to erode, we must talk about it. Withholding only makes it worse because we then usually shut down and withdraw. We can authentically articulate our feelings and concerns from a place of care and respect for the friendship. With a clear understanding of what's expected from each other, we'll both know when trust is being compromised. Then we can take steps to fix things before it's too late and the damage to the relationship is irreparable.

Loyalty: Being There for One Another

"A true friend is there for me when I need her" is one of the common attributes women say they treasure most in friendship. Loyalty is often defined as "unwavering in devotion, unswerving in allegiance, and faithful to commitment or obligation." It means we'll stand by our friend through calm and storm.

"I put a lot of effort into maintaining my friendships and have learned to invest as much as I receive. That means I expect the phone to work both ways," says thirty-five-year-old Patricia, an esthetician. "I expect my friends to be there for me through the good, the bad, and the ugly, and to be candid with me, as I am with them. I cherish a friend who will see me as an individual first, as Patricia, then as a mom, wife, daughter, sister, esthetician, and business owner. I cherish the women who can pick up where we left off with no judgment of time passed, just gratitude to meet up again in the present."

MargE, a twenty-six-year-old woman who works in the family advocacy unit of a military hospital, shares her experience. "I want a friend I can be goofy with," she says. "When I'm with my best friends, I am just ridiculously silly and feel like I am ten years old. I want a friend who knows me and isn't afraid to tell me how she feels, and calls me out on something I might be doing that is out of character. I also want a loyal friend. I can pretty much overlook all other attributes if I know that, at the end of the day, my friend is going to be there no matter what. Another thing that means a lot to me, that goes hand-in-hand with loyalty, is knowing that a friend will stand up for me in my absence. Any time someone has done that for me, it has meant the world to me. I often fall into the protector role for my friends, so when I allow them to protect me, and they actually do, it means a lot!"

When women speak about their strongest friendships, they typically say things like "Regardless of the amount of time that's passed or the physical distance between us, we just seem to pick up where we left off." Time or space doesn't really separate great friends. These are the friends we can count on to "be there for us" no matter what. This "count-on-ability" takes many forms. It can range from literally showing up when a friend's in need to looking out for each other's best interests when making a difficult decision. Whatever count-on-ability is for us, we know when a friend is really in our corner and when she's not. Those who rally when we need them are the friends we hold dearest and, in turn, are the ones we'll drop everything for!

Lynn, 55, believes a true friend is someone who will be there when she calls. Patty did just that when she responded to Lynn's worst nightmare—being attacked by a stranger.

"I had walked home from the synagogue and was just outside my apartment when a man punched me in the chin and took my purse," Lynn says. "A kid heard me scream and helped me inside my apartment. I was single then, and the first person I called on my way to the emergency room was my friend Patty. She lived forty minutes away from me, but she rushed to the ER. As soon as she saw that I was OK, she fainted, and we spent the night in the ER on side-by-side gurneys. Patty and I are very different but very compatible. Our attraction to each other is from our differences, not our similarities. We have so many years of common experiences; it's as if she is a close relative. We hug each other and yell at each other, but we never question the foundation of our relationship."

When times are tough for our friends, are we there for them? Do we stop what we're doing to be by their sides, either literally or figuratively? Loyalty—being there for one another—has many expressions. Underlying it all is the need and desire to have someone we can count on show up when and where we need her.

When Margaret's dearest friend, Eileen, was dying, Margaret dropped everything to be by her side numerous times throughout her cancer journey.

"There was one particularly deep moment when Eileen declined with little hope in sight," says Margaret. "I remember flying from San Diego to St. Louis, my sister driving me to the hospital, and the experience of seeing Eileen in the hospital bed. I sat at her side with my head on her chest saying, 'It wasn't supposed to be this way. You aren't supposed to leave me first!'"

With Margaret's arrival, Eileen's condition improved somewhat, and she was able to go home again. Eileen shared that she didn't want to die without Margaret's being there.

"I had a two-week trip to India planned and made Eileen promise she wouldn't die while I was away," says Margaret. "Soon after returning to San Diego to pack, I got a call that her condition had worsened. Asking the caregiver to hold the phone to Eileen's ear, I told her it was OK for her to leave now, that I was there with her no matter what the distance. That night, Eileen passed on."

Unfortunately, we spoke to a number of women who discovered that the friends they thought they could count on disappeared when things got particularly tough, be it suffering an illness, losing a partner, or feeling the insult of a dashed dream. These fair-weather friends are by our sides when things are going well, but when life heads south for us, so do they.

"Don't stop connecting with your friends when the going gets tough," says Linda, a sixty-something professional photographer. "Stick with them. If a friend's going through something, pick up the phone and figure out a time to meet and talk. When you're the one struggling, it's so much nicer when someone calls to check on you. It's harder to be the one reaching out and asking for support."

Linda witnessed her many friends dwindle to just a few after she lost her sister to breast cancer and later suffered a serious health problem herself. "There's nothing harder than to see people falling away because being your friend is too difficult," she says. "To me, true friends are there in good times and bad. They don't write you off just because you can't engage the way you once did. Loyal friends are in the here and now with you, no matter what that takes. Their friendships are not based on circumstances or on what you can do physically. They value what you offer mentally and spiritually, and how you grow together in the process of each new discovery."

Years ago, a horrible car accident left Margaret in varying stages of a body cast for almost a year. During this extremely trying period, her longtime friend Tammy disappeared—even though she and Margaret had been very involved in each other's life. Margaret had supported Tammy in her corporate travels with little things, such as taking in the mail and watering the plants. When little emergencies arose, Tammy would call Margaret for a favor. After the long recovery, Margaret invited Tammy and her husband over for dinner. Tammy commented that she was glad things were back to normal, because Margaret had just been too depressed for her to be around. At that moment, Margaret realized there was no real friendship between them. While she smiled politely on the outside, mentally she flipped Tammy off. Tammy hadn't been there when Margaret needed her most, and Margaret was no longer willing to be in such a lopsided relationship.

We also want friends cheering us on to greatness. "You can do it!" "I believe in you." These women accept us for who we are and who we want to be. They're not caught up in jealousy because they have their own dreams and know we'll provide the same kind of unwavering support for them.

While we can't necessarily make ourselves available 24-7, we can find ways to champion our friends. This may mean supporting a friend's goal to exercise, stick to a healthy diet, see her child off to college without falling apart, or finally get into counseling. We're there to provide motivation, guidance, and support.

Have you ever sent out an SOS to a friend? Diane did just that when, after talking to her son late one evening, she realized Kevin needed tutoring to pass his EMT course. Diane got up early and went online to look for tutors. When she had to leave for work and still wasn't satisfied with what she'd found, she emailed an SOS to her close friend Noonie who works from home. Within hours Noonie found an EMT instructor she could sense would be perfect for Kevin—and later Kevin passed the national registry exam. Diane will forever be indebted to Noonie who rushed in with heart to save the day!

G✸TCHA! MOMENT

How to Let Others Contribute to You

It's easy to want to be at your friend's side when she needs help. Are you equally generous in letting your friends contribute to you when you need help? Do you justify not reaching out by saying things to yourself like:

✸ "I can handle this; I'm not weak."

✸ "I don't want to bother friends with my troubles."

✸ "This is too embarrassing. What will people think?"

✸ "I don't want my friend to think badly of my (husband, child, or boss)."

✸ "This will pass; I'll hold on until it gets better."

When you hear this kind of self-talk, take it as an opportunity to deepen your friendships. Get on the horn and let your friends be friends!

Transparency and Authenticity: Being Who We Say We Are

We all want a place where we can be ourselves with those who know us best. Intimacy allows for a deep level of communication and relatedness. Being genuine with our friends provides an opening for them to be *real* with us in return. So what does it take to achieve transparency and authenticity in our friendships?

Anne Marie, 78, a partner in her husband's dental practice, says she knows when she's met a woman with whom she can be honest and open. "This woman is not focused on being *interesting* but is *interested* in me," she explains. "She's concerned about me and what matters in my life.

There are so many situations in life where we have to be careful and on guard. Consider it a treasured gift if you have a friend you trust enough to say what's really in your heart and on your mind, without fear of being judged or having your confidence broken."

To Janelle, 30, a special education teacher, a true friend is someone who makes her a better person. She seeks friends who have the courage to say things she may not want to hear and vice versa.

"For some that's a deal breaker," she says. "Honesty can cause friction, but a sincere friend is willing to listen. I believe that being direct, confronting things, and moving on is more beneficial than avoiding problems. When I speak up, I remind my friends that I'm doing so because I love them. I might ask a question like, 'Are you sure this is the best scenario?'

"That doesn't mean it's easy. My twin sister, Brittany, and my good friends have let me have it when they've needed to be straight with me. As women, we may need time to reflect and think about things. So we're good about giving each other space and coming back together after we've processed the information. For me taking a walk or doing something active is the best way to talk things through. We know we will all be in each other's weddings, be there for the birth of our children, and be in it for the long haul."

We create a sacred space in our friendships when we give each other the gift of authenticity. It allows us to say what's really there for us and allows our friend to hear it without assessment, judgment, or evaluation. We might feel this kind of transparency is only achievable with a few special women, but that doesn't have to be so. If we focus on bringing more and more women into our innermost circle, we expand this sacred space in our lives. Our opportunities to give and receive grow with exponential rewards.

So if we long to be real with our friends and have them reciprocate, what gets in our way? Pretense! When we pretend, we create a barrier between ourselves and others. It's as if we put on a cloak to cover up who we really are. These cloaks of inauthentic behavior can be bold and obnoxious or subtle and even endearing, but hide us nonetheless. Haven't we all put on the "nice" cloak, the "I've got it all handled" cloak, or the "that doesn't bother me" cloak? When we do, we're in a game of pretense. That's when women say, "I can't relate to her." The end result is separation.

The cloak of "fake-it" behavior is always easier to spot on someone else. We meet a woman we want to get to know, but the "fake-it cloak" keeps us at a superficial level. The tone is pleasant, polite, and in control—never ruffled, disappointed, or angry. This front, regardless of the amount of time we spend together, doesn't let us get to know each other at a deep and satisfying level. In fact, it can seem off-putting. We all know that life isn't perfect, but when we pretend it is, we seem disingenuous and unrelated to the other person. No one wants to trust her inner world with someone who doesn't seem *of* this world. Being real is key. It may seem risky in the moment, but the potential pay-off is high.

Sharing from a place of openness and trust often begets an "I know what you mean" response and the sharing of a similar experience or feeling. This immediately tells us she's on the same plane we're on and not in a "perfect-life" stratosphere with no idea of what we're going through. Our friend is there *with* us, almost symbiotic in our joy or pain.

Diane found that when she risked opening up about real-life issues, women reciprocated in turn.

"For years, I didn't think I could share too much about my personal life," says Diane. "But when I did reveal the challenges along with the successes, and didn't act like I had it all together, my friends didn't have to pretend to be perfect either. When we're transparent and real, women sense it. They know they can trust us with their 'baggage'—even if it's a small carry-on compared to our heavy trunks!"

If Diane had decided it all was just too personal and private to share, she wouldn't have the close relationships she enjoys today.

Have we been real with our friends? If not, it may be time to test the water and see what happens. We can share a little something, and see how our friends react. If they're truly there for us, we'll feel supported in our vulnerability. In fact, they'll rally and let us know we're not alone. They might even share something similar from their own experiences to let us know they relate. Those are "I know what you mean" kinds of friends.

Listening: So Others Can Be Heard

For many of us, sharing is the easy part. It's the shutting up and listening to our friend that's tough. It can be especially hard to listen to the whole story without jumping to the rescue with suggestions or advice. We may be surprised, aghast, annoyed, or disappointed. If we want to protect the friendship, let's think about how we respond before blurting out our feelings or advice. We can ask our friend what she wants from us at that moment. What would be most helpful? We can find out if she's interested in hearing our perspective. Does she want advice now, or does she just want us to listen?

In a program on partnership, Margaret learned to practice the "partnership pause." This "pause" involves taking a moment, maybe counting to five, and thinking about our response before reacting. Some women naturally rely on the partnership pause; others may benefit from practice.

Margaret has been told that she doesn't have a poker face—the ability to not react in a way that reveals what cards she's holding in her hand (or the feelings in her heart). Not having a poker face can result in some real momentary altercations. Haven't we all experienced the look of surprise, disappointment, or even disapproval when we've said something that a friend doesn't agree with or approve of? While such nonverbal cues could be seen as complete transparency, wouldn't it be easier if we practiced the partnership pause and took stock of the situation? This gives us time to ask ourselves, "What does my friend really need from me right now?" "Is this the time to let it all out?" "How can I speak the truth in a way that will not diminish or embarrass my friend?" The partnership pause fosters open and honest communication that's helpful, not hurtful, and results in an even "safer" friendship space. The "pause" allows us to think before we speak, which is listening of the very best kind.

"There is a certain quality of listening among true friends that allows you to just be there for the other," says Cynthia, 50, a business consultant. "The best kind of listening is when you can just be present with your friend, listening to learn with a sense of empathy and a desire to understand."

One of Cynthia's friends, Fay, had a tragic family situation in which a young relative overdosed on drugs. When Fay called "to talk," Cynthia could hear that something was "off" in Fay's voice. Rather than asking what was wrong, she listened carefully while waiting for her friend to open up.

"I've come to realize that when I'm listening, I don't always have to say or do something immediately," says Cynthia.

The partnership pause served both Cynthia and Fay. Cynthia didn't press or prod; she just let Fay talk. When, in her own time, Fay shared what was happening in her life, Cynthia supported her in a genuine, caring way.

Women are blessed with a special kind of listening acumen. It's a real gift we give to each other. With focused listening, our friendships emerge in a variety of ways and grow with many possibilities. As we share stories and get to know each other, our relationships deepen. The closer we listen and the more we reveal who we are and what we're facing, the stronger the bonds. Our friendships are firmly planted.

Reciprocation: The Responsibility to Give Back

Friendship is reciprocal, but it's not always equal. Some days we may feel like we're the one always having to take the lead and exert extra effort. Other days we may be the one receiving more than we give. When we're inside of a friendship based on mutual care and trust, does it matter who's extending and who's receiving? Real friendship is not about keeping score. Just being mindful of the value of reciprocating will let us know when it's time to return the favor. We might drive to her place, pay for the coffee, acknowledge a birthday, or send a thank-you note.

Thinking everything has to be even or fair can strain a friendship. Just because we bought our friend a gift for the holidays, we shouldn't expect a gift in return. Let's allow our friends to reciprocate in a way that works for them and be thankful.

But what happens when things are one-sided? What do we do when we don't experience reciprocity, and we want it? If we believe a relationship is lopsided—that we're engaging much more than our friend—it's easy to feel slighted and bitter. This dis-ease in us is a signal to communicate how we feel rather than letting our frustration eat away at the relationship.

Likewise, when we find ourselves mostly on the receiving end and know we can't return the favor, it's another signal to authentically communicate. We can verbally appreciate all she's doing and share that we don't have the resources (money, time, energy) to reciprocate in the same way. If we're honest yet thoughtful in how we phrase things, she'll be more likely to understand.

Many years ago when Margaret's sister Barbara was struggling financially, she would accept a dinner invitation by saying that she was happy to go out but didn't have the money to buy a meal. Splitting an appetizer and sharing each other's company was what she could do. This level of authenticity gave her friends a choice, and they, in turn, were accommodating and gracious. Today Barbara is able to repay her friends who so lovingly supported her years ago by treating *them* to dinner.

Giving back isn't always about an even exchange of time and money. Appreciation is a gift in itself! When we receive a gift or an act of kindness, making a big deal over what our friend has done for us can be the best way to return the favor.

"I cherish it when my friends lean on me for advice or insight," says Deborah, 48, a retained executive search consultant. "And if they need that over and over again, I am fine with it because I know I've relied on them, and they've been there for me in the past. Sometimes we need to take 90 percent and give 10 percent. The reward comes when they seek me out to say thank you and tell me how things have changed. It makes me feel good when someone I care about has made headway because of my help. It means I've allowed her to take a deep breath for a moment and rely on me. And that feels great."

G⁜TCHA! MOMENT

Asking for What You Want

In a moment of crisis, how do you let your friends know what you need from them and the kind of support that will really help you? Don't make your friends guess. Be direct. Let them know *how* to help you. "I really need your advice. I want to tell you what happened first, and then I'd like your suggestions." Or "I need to vent. Would you mind just listening?" If you don't say what you want, you could get what you *don't* want and then become angry with your friends. How fair is that?

Accountability: Holding Each Other Responsible to Our Values

Many women value and appreciate accountability in their friendships. With permission, we can help each other *do* what we say we want to do or *be* who we say we want to be. When we recognize that a girlfriend is not behaving in a way that will serve her best interest, we let her know. We do so out of love, and in a way that allows her to maintain dignity.

Patty, 48, a vice president of quality for a health system, seeks friends who help her be true to herself and live her values. "Through relationship challenges, career changes, or child-rearing issues, my friend Michele tells me exactly what she thinks without any filter because she loves me," says Patty. "We all have blind spots, and the directness of 'I know you and you're not being all you can be' helps me not compromise."

To Patty, authentic dialogue separates friends from acquaintances. "It's not just about what's going great, but what we're really scared about, challenged by, or in pain over," says Patty. "These conversations create a bond and community."

A criterion for friendship, especially for those in our innermost circle, is being able to tell the truth and have our friends serve as mirrors for us. When we're not thinking clearly or acting rationally, they're the ones who have the courage to tell us. They're not afraid to point out a blind spot and call attention to something that we may see or choose to ignore. These friends are willing to take a risk and ask the tough questions. They're able to *hang out* in the uncertainty of not knowing how it will all *turn out*. It requires a huge commitment to the person and the friendship to take this kind of stand.

Ellen, 60, a branding specialist and speaker, says her friend Deb is someone she can count on to help her live life with integrity. "I'm strong, independent, and a real optimist," says Ellen. "I'm the one who helps everyone else through their problems. But that strength means that when I can't handle something, some of my friends say, 'Uh-oh, if Ellen can't handle it, we're not sure we can help.' I've gone through losing the love of my life to cancer and suffering from uterine cancer myself. Even though I'm strong, I appreciate someone who will let me be a victim for awhile.

"My friend Deb allows me to whine and have a pity party, but only for awhile. One day when I was feeling very down, she and I were talking by phone, and she said, 'This is not what you need to do right now!' Because she's been so understanding, the directness of her words snapped me right out of my whining, and I got back to making positive things happen."

While we're never sure how someone will receive our input, the way we deliver the message is key. Being aware of *why* we're saying something will help us be conscious of *how* we say it. If our goal is to make a contribution to our friend or support her, we'll be selective in choosing the right words. We may want to prepare her listening by stating our intention and what we're committed to. We might say, "I don't know exactly how to say this, but I care about you, and I'm going to tell you something that may be hard to hear. Is that OK?"

It's better to say what we need to say than hold back and have our behavior speak for us. As long as we act out of good intentions, we can make a mess and clean it up later. Wouldn't we rather have a friend who's willing to take a bold stand for us, even if it's upsetting, than someone who settles for a shallow relationship?

"I appreciate friends who are good at demonstrating caring and who can be vulnerable and peel back the onion to go deeper," says Margie, 70, a leadership coach. "I want friends who are willing to trust me and be led by me while knowing I am not judging them. Likewise, I treasure friends who want the best for me."

So when it's our turn to accept feedback from a trusted friend, how can we respond and not shoot the messenger? Avoiding a "how dare you say that" attitude will allow us to really hear what our friend has to say. This may mean putting aside our defenses and simply saying, "I hear you, and I want some time to think about what you've said." Or "That never even occurred to me. Thank you."

When women we respect tell us the truth, it can force us to confront things that, deep inside, we know we've been avoiding. Their insight and perspective help us see through our delusions and excuses. It's a reckoning that brings us to a new place where we can find the resolve to take actions that move us in a healthier direction.

When all is said and done, women want women of character to be their friends. We want friends who are there for the long haul. They care beyond our stupid moments, offer a helping hand when we fall down, and forgive us when we screw up. We crave friends who know us so well they can finish our thoughts and sentences. With these special women, we feel a connection of the heart that allows for an understanding state of mind. They "get" us. And they provide a safe place where we can be ourselves, let it all out, and know that our conversation is held sacred. It's in the vault.

Fun: Laughter Bonds

Whether it's laughing with our friends or laughing at ourselves, women appreciate levity. We like to be with friends who allow us to feel comfortable enough to let our hair down and forget our worries—at least for a time. In other words, sometimes we simply want to have fun.

Laughing is good for our health. It exercises our diaphragm, contracts our abs, and works out our heart and shoulders, leaving muscles more relaxed. According to WebMD, laughter increases blood flow and infection-fighting antibodies as well as boosts our immune cells. It also releases endorphins—the body's feel-good hormone—and painkiller. Because laughter is often social, it's not clear if the health improvements come from being with friends and family or the act of laughing itself. Whichever it is, laughing improves the quality of our lives.

Humor binds us together, increases happiness and intimacy, and even heals hurts, according the Helpguide.org. This website calls laughter the "antidote to stress" because it reduces pain and conflict. Humor lightens our burdens, inspires hope, keeps us grounded, and brings our mind and body back into balance.

Lightening things up is also a way to find new perspective. The lens of humor takes us away from the "everyday-ness" of life. We see things in a new light and don't take ourselves so seriously. Looking at things differently doesn't change reality, but it can help us view our life and problems in positive ways.

While arranging their schedules to write this book, Diane told Margaret that her husband, Matt, calls her a "day stuffer" because of all the activities she tries to fit into twenty-four hours. They laughed hysterically. Why? Because Margaret suffers from the same day-stuffing malady. They discussed their penchant for cramming too much in and how different they were from their take-it-as-it-comes husbands. Perhaps they could tone it down a bit and fill their calendars less. A good laugh. A good lesson.

Lolma, 61, a leader in organizational transformation work, remembers her best friend Deena, who died from cancer, for the fun and laughter they shared. "There was something so special about our friendship because she made everyday things funny," says Lolma fondly. "Deena could get me to go to the depths of myself and then to the heights of what I knew I could be. She allowed me and her other friends to see the best in life, and she used humor to get us there."

To have this kind of joy in our relationships, we must be present to it. In other words, we need to give ourselves and the women in our lives permission to get a little crazy. Pure, unadulterated girl fun allowed here. Laughing out loud preferred. Wanting to do fun things expected!

Margaret and her friends gave each other the green light to have crazy fun when they sailed a catamaran in Greece. "We read animal medicine cards, the Native American version of Tarot cards, and played Mexican Train Wreck, a game with special domino-like cards. We just acted silly and forgot about reality for awhile."

So let's take time to have fun with our girlfriends. Share a whimsical thought or embarrassing moment. Reveal something stupid you or someone else said. Gab about a foible. Tell a joke or two. In other words, unleash your sense of humor.

G✵TCHA! MOMENT

Girls Just Want to Have Fun!

Need an extra push to laugh? Try these:

- ✺ See a funny chick flick, go to a comedy act, or watch a hilarious YouTube video or sitcom.
- ✺ Invite girlfriends out to lunch with one request: They must bring a joke or two. Tell the jokes, and watch how the laughter rolls.
- ✺ Go people-watching at the beach or park, or head to the nearest Ferris wheel or merry-go-round.
- ✺ Dare a friend to run through the sprinklers on an afternoon walk, or go out and take a turn at karaoke.

It's good for us to let go and loosen up. We'll discover a different kind of teasing and scheming than when we're with our partners and children—and it's supposed to be that way. It's girl time!

G✺TCHA! MOMENT

What a Friend Is and Isn't to You

Write down the qualities you most admire and desire in a friend. Use your list to start a conversation with a friend to explore her preferences and reveal yours. Your discussion can help you identify each other's key friendship attributes and reset expectations and boundaries. Being clear about "what a friend is and isn't" is an important way-finder in our journey to satisfying and meaningful female relationships.

Chapter 4

Diversifying Our Friendship Portfolio

When we examine our circle of friends, we might see women who think, act, and even look just like us. We often believe a real friend is our mirror image and as comfortable to be with as wearing a nicely worn-in shoe. If we are outgoing and gregarious or quiet and subdued, aren't we attracted to the same kind of women? Do we assume that if a woman's life is pretty much like ours, we can more easily connect at a soul level? "But I have friends who are opposite from me," we say. Scratch a little deeper. Aren't they really more the same than different? We may be outgoing and they may be shy, but chances are we often share many other traits with our friends, like the same socio-economic status, age group, and culture.

So, let's spice it up! Women who aren't exactly like us add texture to our lives. Whether it's a variety of ethnicities, religions, belief systems, ages, or marital and career status, mixing up our circle of friends exposes us to differences that allow for new perspectives. Opening our hearts and minds to a variety of women encourages us to go down new paths, sing new songs, and pray new prayers. Because these friends are different from us, they often approach life from a unique vantage point. With a healthy curiosity, we can gain new dimension in our lives and benefit from all they've experienced.

If we only hang out with people similar to us, our lives will continue to have the same ol' look and feel. A black-and-white world can get pretty boring if we're not willing to add a splash of color here and there. Variety definitely adds flavor to our lives.

Moving Beyond Our Mirror Image

"I see that I have a firmly held belief that I can't really be friends with people more successful than I am," says Donna, 54, a hairstylist. "Whether it's their finances, relationships, health, career, or other important areas of life, I feel inferior in their presence and don't think I have anything to offer them."

What a courageous thing for Donna to say! Her truthfulness is refreshing and may be what many of us have thought as well. Yet, we sometimes don't consider all we have to offer the women we see as more successful. Our perspectives, experiences, and insights may be just what others need to open their world and solve their problems. All may not be as it appears on the surface.

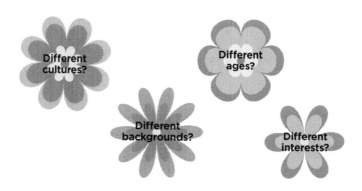

Making new friends who are not our mirror image may take effort. Understanding and even expecting that we may initially feel outside our comfort zone will help us get through any awkward or uncomfortable moments. It just takes one connection point to open up a conversation that leads to more connections and more conversations. Our commonalities are far greater than our differences. We don't have to look, sound, or dress alike; worship the same; or have similar backgrounds or earning power to be able to relate to one another. It's our humanness and our womanhood that does that for us—thank God.

Making that unlikely friend is a lot like dating. It could be the one that you don't *think* is "your type" who's just the person you need or want in your life.

Barbara, 61, a passionate nutrition and health advocate, met one of her dearest friends twenty years ago at a house-painting party.

"It seemed unlikely that we would become friends because Gail was dating Jerry, and I suspected that he had eyes for me," says Barbara. "She was probably thinking, 'Who's this woman in my territory?' But since we were the only two women who showed up at the party, we couldn't avoid each other. When I said, 'We have to wash this woodwork first,' Gail told me she thought to herself, 'a woman after my own heart.' In that moment, we set aside our fears and concerns and just liked each other. I'm glad we did because that was the beginning of a loving, lasting relationship. Oh, and Jerry? Soon after, he left the picture. Thank goodness we did not let a notion of jealousy spoil our friendship."

Opening our minds and extending some generosity can result in the unexpected and the unimaginable. Isn't that what we want anyway?

Linda, 53, a pharmacist working in sales management, met an unlikely friend in a nail salon. When the two chatted and learned they lived two floors apart in the same building, they started a more in-depth conversation.

"She's the artsy, Bohemian type who owned antique shops and is an interior designer, while I'm the corporate type. She's Jewish; I'm Catholic. She was married in her late twenties, and when she separated, she was more active about dating. I've been single my entire life, and when we go out together dancing, I am ready to go home before midnight while she wants to stay out until 2:00 or 3:00 a.m. But it's our similar values that drew us together and bond our friendship as we navigate life. We're both very spiritual, easy to talk to, and only six months apart in age. We've met each other's families and have been close friends for six years. I supported her through breast cancer and a mastectomy. Even with our differences, there's richness in our relationship. She brings me a different perspective, and for that, I'm very grateful."

Opposites Attract

The kind of "opposites attract" karma that pervades male/female relationships is also at work among girlfriends. We're attracted to something in them that's missing in our own lives. MargE, 26, says, "I have a friend who is my opposite in so many things. I met her through a friend on Facebook five years ago, and we just started chatting back and forth. There are very few things that we actually agree on, such as movies, books, politics, etc. However, there are enough things we see eye to eye on that allow us to find some common ground. Yet we are still different in so many ways. I think that what she sees in me might make her gravitate toward me because we do complement each other well. I love that she reads books and is intelligent, bold, and brave. She is who she is, like it or not. And that's something I admire and respect. Ultimately, we get along even if we don't agree all of the time. Even though I've only been with this friend in person three or four times, she truly is one of my best friends. She always listens to me and genuinely cares about my problems. Despite all of our differences, I'm thankful she's my friend."

Cheryl, 45, says Tracey, her best friend since age twelve, is completely different from her and always has been, yet they are as close as sisters. In high school, Cheryl was academic, athletic, a cheerleader, and prom queen, while Tracey hung out with the "greaser" drug crowd. Today Tracey is a busy property manager, and her husband's a mechanic. Cheryl is a pediatrician, whose husband comes from a wealthy family and loves theater.

"Tracey is a complete slob," says Cheryl. "I can't even stay at her house; it's so filthy and is in constant chaos. She laughs at my uptight housekeeping and thinks my home looks like a museum. Even though our husbands' personalities clash, that hasn't gotten in the way of how we think about each other. Our friendship has its own life. She makes me laugh, and our personalities just mesh. Once a month, we calendar in a nice long lunch and meet halfway between New York and New Jersey. In between meeting we'll call or e-mail, but our lunch is sacred."

Are there women in our lives we're drawn to but haven't reached out to connect with because they seem so unlike us? By allowing ourselves to explore opposite points of view, new and even unlikely friendships can evolve. It's definitely worth a try!

G✳TCHA! MOMENT

What Opposite Do You Want to Attract?

One friend can't fulfill everything for you. Take a few minutes to think about how you might diversify your friendship portfolio. Ask yourself:

- ✳ What interests do I have that I lack friends to share them with?
- ✳ Do I have friends who represent a variety of cultures, religious beliefs, lifestyles, or backgrounds?
- ✳ Am I receptive to women who are younger or older than I am?
- ✳ Is it OK if she doesn't work outside the home and I do? Or vice versa?
- ✳ Can I be friends with someone who is staff when I'm in management?

You can create opportunities to meet women of different cultures, lifestyles, careers, ages, and interests. Seize the moment to engage in conversations or step into situations that could lead to a friendship. You can break the ice by asking questions such as: "What are you passionate about?" "What do you love about your life?" "What lights you up?" Awareness, intention, and attention are the first steps to fulfilling our dreams. Dream big and dream wide!

Learning from Our Differences

One of the most rewarding aspects of an unlikely friendship is seeing life from a different vantage point, especially if we can share openly.

Allison, 38, says when she started going out with her new friend Liz she wasn't sure they could be friends. Allison openly shared her emotions, but Liz was quiet and rarely revealed her feelings. Allison didn't know where she stood and feared Liz was judging her.

"My mom reminded me that Liz was raised in a strict Persian family. Sharing emotions and feelings was probably new to her. I realized that, although we both lived in New York, we had a cultural divide. We kept doing things together, however, and finally she let her personality break through. That really humanized her for me. Today Liz is a close friend. She's always reading something interesting and challenging me intellectually. We have so many differences, yet our common interests bring us together. We both love running, other cultures, and great restaurants. I now seek diversity in my friendships. I see people as people, not as their culture or religion. If you're human and interesting, I want to learn more. Thank God I live in a melting pot."

Allison's willingness to move beyond the early awkward moments resulted in a lasting and rewarding friendship. Her initial curiosity and intrigue supported Allison in following her heart. Both women remained tenacious in their desire to know each other better. Getting out of their comfort zones resulted in a breakthrough that allowed these two women to reap the benefits of friendship.

Donna, 53, a European-American, had always considered herself an open person with respect to friends. When she joined a group of doctoral students that included five African-Americans, an Israeli national, a Mexican national, two lesbians, a bisexual woman, and one gay man, she became exposed to diversity in a big way.

"I now refer to that time in my educational experience as the year to develop cross-cultural understanding," says Donna.

That experience opened in Donna a deep desire to have all sorts of different friends that she could learn from, mentor, and support.

"I remember sitting on a fence with one of the African-American women telling her about growing up in Texas in the 1960s. I had asked an African-American girl to go swimming with me, but she wasn't allowed at the pool. My study partner told me that because of segregation, a lot of African-American women don't know how to swim. As we grew closer, I learned that her fifteen-year-old daughter had drowned and immediately assumed it was because she didn't know how to swim. Later, I learned that her daughter had been on the high school swim team and had gotten caught in the current swimming in some caves. I learned how wrong assumptions about others could be. Diverse friendships have broadened my consciousness. It's given me more compassion and a better ability to put myself in others' shoes. I'm now able to better understand the multifaceted texture of life.

"Our friendship lasted well beyond our doctorate program. We both learned to trust more and tell the truth even if feelings got hurt. But what's been most interesting is that our trust in each other has also given us the security to know that if we say something stupid about race, the other will understand that the intention was honorable."

If we love expanding our horizons, we'll seek out women different from us. The lessons will be life changing!

Opening Our Minds Creates Common Ground

It's easier to be with women who are just like us, but it takes openness and generosity to be with someone *unlike* us. All friendships begin with a background of relatedness. It's interesting to think of the possibility of friendship based on who we are "with" in the moment. What can we enjoy about her now? What can we learn today?

Lolma, 61, says that she has met many women who don't share her politics or religion, but it doesn't matter to her anymore.

"I love them for exactly who they are," she says. "We connect where we connect—often at our values and our belief in God, not in a religious way but spiritually," she says.

Lolma says her marriage to her wife has turned out to be a non-issue with her friends. "Earlier in my life, when I saw things more in black and white, I sometimes restricted who I was going to become friends with," she says. "That way of thinking limited me. So I opened myself up more. My work in health care is about leaving assumptions and judgments behind. I had to ask myself if I was doing that personally. Today I let my friends be exactly who they are. And I wait until I am sure someone really likes me before I share all of who I am. Then I know they will care about me in a whole way."

We can think of our friendships as a kaleidoscope and not limit ourselves to one view. Imagine the kind of treasures we'll discover and add to our lives, if we don't always have to be doing the same kind of things with the same kind of people.

"I challenge myself to be open to differences, and sometimes it's not a conscious decision; I just happen to click with that person," says Deborah, 48. "Adding someone new to your mix of friends teaches you a lot about yourself and others. It lets you learn and grow."

With the unique characteristics and backgrounds each of us brings, we'll see different facets of ourselves. We can think of our new relationships as an evolution and allow ourselves to be present and feel "complete" in the moment with these friends. In the process, we can shift our mindsets from "me" driving the relationships to "us" creating them. From this viewpoint, the possibilities are endless.

Marie, 50, moved with her husband from Toronto, Canada, to Detroit, Michigan, to advance his career in the auto industry. His job took him to South America every other week. Alone half the time, Marie had to focus on how to make it in a new country, new city, and new neighborhood. She befriended her neighbor Carrie, who had left her law practice to open up a Pilates fitness institute.

"I was not a fitness person," says Marie. "I was uncoordinated and had no rhythm, but I needed friends, so I went to the Pilates group. Not only did I grow closer to Carrie, but I met all sorts of women—from entrepreneurs to stay-at-home moms. It was fun to get to know them and experience a new kind of fitness. Now I'm a huge Pilates disciple and have even opened my mind to yoga. Growing more coordinated and fit has made me a better person. I believe that when your body is in shape, your mind is also in shape. I never would have these wonderful practices in my life if I hadn't taken Carrie up on her offer to do something outside my comfort zone."

Later through yoga, Marie met Susan, who had also recently relocated to Detroit to get married after a long career at the telephone company Bell Canada.

"Although we are both very different, we discovered our common Canadian heritage and a passion for traveling and world culture," says Marie. "In a quest to find her next professional adventure, Susan enrolled for three months in an organic culinary school in Ireland. During her summer in Ireland, we stayed in touch, often discussing nutrition and raw food preparations. Upon her return to Detroit, she hosted an organic food dinner paired with wonderful wines. Later, when Susan moved to Chicago, Illinois, we connected though e-mail, phone conversations, and snail mail—whatever it took—and got together for long weekends in Chicago. We share books, advice, ideas, and laughter. We always support each other. Susan's different perspective allows me to consider another point of view, which I value."

Marie is an example of someone who pursued friendship even though the potential friend didn't fit her personal mold. "Often new relationships start at a superficial level," says Marie. "But I know that if I want a friendship to have depth, it's up to me to groom it and invest in it, just as I would my finances and my career. I try to be open to new experiences and add to the relationship in any way I can."

Even when we think we're very different from a potential new friend, by sticking with it we can usually find common ground. We often see something to admire or learn. In the process, we become stronger, more open, and even grateful that our differences make the world a magical and interesting place.

Fifty-three-year-old Sandye, an executive assistant, says she's the curious type, and that helps her approach women different from her. "In my workplace, I reached out to a woman from India, and we started going to a fitness center. When she returned from a month's visit to India, she brought me back a sari and taught me how to wear it—what a bonding experience!

"Girlfriends are my strength and resource. I appreciate women of all types," Sandye continues. "They support me, help me, tell me the truth, and guide me through life's journey, which can be really difficult at times. I have a number of very good friends, but I'm always in a friend-making mode."

Broadening our friendship perspective means taking risk. When we do, we expand our minds and our worlds.

G❋TCHA! MOMENT

Getting Out of the Box

Taking action outside of your normal way of doing things is one way to diversify your friendship portfolio. Consider that if it's uncomfortable you might be on the right track. Here are a few things to try:

* ❀ Do something out of *your* ordinary, be it attending a roller derby or high tea.
* ❀ Join a group that will make you stretch. Seek out opportunities that are civic, philanthropic, religious, or social.
* ❀ Volunteer in your community or for a special event.
* ❀ Train for a breast cancer walk.
* ❀ Expand your conversation on an airplane or train beyond chitchat.
* ❀ Reach out to someone younger or older. Explore how your lives could connect.

Another State of Life—Does It Really Matter?

Women in another "state of life" can offer us what we don't currently have in our own life. Marital and child status don't need to be barriers between friends. While single women relate more immediately with other single women, whether single, married, mother or not, there are many other connecting points that we can consciously find and act upon.

Liz, 54, is single and lives miles away from her relatives. Maggie and her husband, Roger, are Liz's "family away from family" on Boston's south shore.

"That's where I go every year to blow out my birthday candles," says Liz. "When my mother was still alive, she always joined me at Maggie's home for the holiday, as it was also my mom's birthday. Maggie knew that, as much as I would have liked to, I couldn't have managed the entire day alone with my mother. Maggie played the third-party buffer so we could be together and fully enjoy one another's company and that of others."

Being married or single really has nothing to do with whether or not we can be there for each other. That comes from the heart, not from the presence or absence of a wedding band.

"I've been single since my adult triplets were toddlers, yet 90 percent of my friends are married, living with someone, or gay with partners," says Shellie, 65, an executive recruiter. "I've never felt like a third wheel. In fact when my good friend Meryl is traveling, I may go out to dinner with her son and fiancé. Likewise, I can get on the phone with my friend Carol's husband and talk for hours. Since I don't have many relatives, my friends have become my family."

Imagine what Shellie's life would be like if she only connected with other single women. Her ability to act outside her mirror image has allowed for a rich array of friends. Befriending only women like us shrinks our opportunities for plentiful and stimulating lives. If we understand that "being" female is our common bond, we will pursue opening ourselves to women who *seem* different. Chances are we'll connect more than we thought possible.

Ellen, 60, who's been married twice, relies on all her friends—no matter what their life stage. "Girlfriends have saved my life," she says. "With lots of loss, hardship, and major health issues, I'd be in a padded room drooling if not for girlfriends."

When doctors diagnosed Ellen with stage III uterine cancer, she had to wait a month before her surgeon was available. "I lived in a trance during those four weeks," she says. "However, I continued working and giving presentations to clients. I acted as though nothing was wrong.

"My every-other-day phone call with Susan, my thirty-year friend in Arizona, was what saved me. Susan is divorced with three children, including a special-needs daughter, while I am childless. My mother couldn't provide the nurturing I needed during my illness, and she wouldn't travel to be at my side for my surgery, yet Susan did. When I thought I couldn't go on, this friend held my hand, reminding me how strong I was and how elegantly I'd handled other crises in my life. Susan is always telling me that she doesn't have any friends as remarkable as I am. I'm so grateful for that kind of affirmation."

What's Age Got to Do With It?

Remember the group you hung out with in high school? They were probably your same age and in your same grade. We rarely made friends with girls younger than we were. That same pattern can follow us as adults. We connect most readily with women our own age, but why not with older women next door or younger moms at the gym?

Janelle, 30, has established a unique and special friendship with Karen, 52, and Fran, 62. They met on a trip with their husbands to attend a college football game. While hanging out and spending quality time together for a few days, Janelle admired the two women's strong bond and later learned that both Karen and Fran had lost their husbands at an early age.

"I told my husband about their neat relationship and support system," says Janelle. "They helped me to realize that bad things can happen to really good people; it's how you respond that matters. I have been inspired by their fighting spirit and hope for the future. They made me appreciate the close friends I have even more. I love spending time with those two women!"

Similarly, Linda, 53, shares her experience to help guide younger women.

"I'm in a professional organization, and younger women seek me out for advice and insight," says Linda. "A young woman asked about mentoring advice that she thought was unique to her generation. I responded that her questions related to where she was in her career (early stages) versus a generational difference (Gen X versus Baby Boomer). I shared that I experienced the same challenges and frustrations to move ahead in my career. The only differences between us are our hairstyles, skirt lengths, and heel heights."

Avoiding age stereotyping allows us to experience the satisfaction that comes from interacting with women half or twice our age. By opening our lives to women of all ages, our worlds expand exponentially. Could a thirty-two-year-old teach an eighty-year-old to text message her grandkids? Could a seventy-five-year-old shut-in become the confidant of a forty-five-year-old volunteer?

Noonie, 51, a freelance writer, remembers her grandmother Iris saying, "I'm shocked when I look in the mirror and see an old lady. You and I relate so well that I feel like we could be college roommates. We are gals, and what's important is we can be who we really are with each other."

It's ironic that grandmothers and granddaughters or mothers and daughters can be best friends, but two unrelated women, decades apart, may feel awkward striking up a friendship. Inter-generational friendships fill voids. Whether our own mothers have passed and we long for a mother figure, or we missed the experience of having daughters, exploring friendship with a woman who fills that role can be deeply satisfying.

"I have friends younger and way older than I am, and I love the view from all angles," says Chris, a baby boomer and single mom. "Experiencing friends across multiple generations is big for me. I love going out with a small group of women ages thirty to sixty. Our conversations give us a glimpse of the past and the future; they allow us to learn from one another. I don't want to only be surrounded by people who think the same way I do."

Kelley, 24, a small business owner and stay-at-home mom, says the first time she spoke to Paige, 39, she instantly knew she wanted to be friends, despite their age difference.

"It seems like an odd introduction, but the first time I met Paige, she apologized to me. She said, 'I judged you before I even met you. I was told all these really good things about you,' and I thought, 'No way. Someone *that* young can't possibly be so wise or have such high standards for her life.' I was sure they were exaggerating. But, within the first minute of meeting you, I could tell I was totally wrong.'

"The fact that Paige, a complete stranger at the time, was willing to humble herself and apologize for being judgmental made me trust her and want to be her friend," says Kelley. "Now a few years later, I've had my first child; and Paige, who has children of her own, is one of my accountability partners. If I am struggling with something, I call her to seek her advice and wisdom. I know that she will be honest with me.

"I have always had a heart for seeking out wisdom," says Kelley. "Those who have lived longer and gone through more than I have can teach me so much. Why go through unnecessary suffering when I can avoid it by learning from those who have gone before me? Likewise, I make it a priority to pass along what I have learned to others so they can avoid making the same mistakes I did."

Kelley realized that, although she's younger, there are life lessons she can pass on to those who are older than she is. Before the birth of her first baby, Kelley confided to her friend Stefanie that she and her husband were making changes to be a better example to their children. A few weeks later, Stefanie and her husband implemented those same changes in their family.

"It made me feel great that they considered what we were doing," says Kelley. "Wisdom is wisdom, no matter how old you are!"

When Lael, 79, moved to Wapiti, Wyoming, she missed her three granddaughters in California. One year Lael invited six neighborhood girls, ranging in age from two to six, to her log cabin for a tea party using orange demitasse cups she bought in Italy. Over the years the Orange Cup Girls' activities grew from playing dress-up to ice-skating parties.

"Once a year, we'd invite all thirty-seven girls and boys in town to a festival," explains Lael. "The Orange Cup Girls would decorate booths representing each holiday, from Valentine's and St. Patrick's Day to Halloween and Christmas. The girls made food and created dances; it was quite a serious production," Lael laughs. "It brought me such joy to be part of their lives. Now they're all grown up and off to college or seeing the world, and we still keep in touch. They are gorgeous creatures inside and out!"

Imagine the knowledge and insight the Orange Cup Girls gained over their years with Lael. It's that same kind of wisdom Sandye, 53, gleans from ninety-nine-year-old Gladys, who she calls her "church mom." Sandye met Gladys at church when she and her own mother were going through a difficult period. They sit together during church services, and Sandye frequently visits Gladys at the retirement home.

"She took me under her wing, and I've been there ever since," says Sandye. "Gladys has outlived four husbands and most of her friends. She reminds me that she's made every mistake and brings me serious wisdom. When I turned forty, she made me feel so young. When she lost her driving privileges, I helped her process the loss. We have a spiritual connection. A lot of times younger people shy away from older ones. Gladys doesn't have any children of her own, so I bring my granddaughter to visit her. It's great to see the joy in her eyes."

Similarly Margie, who is in her seventies, enjoys a friendship with her mom's friend Virginia, who's ninety-four years old. "She's such an interesting person," says Margie. "At age eighty-five, she created a fashion show in which the women wore boxes from the neck down. Each woman decorated her box in a hat, gloves, or a fancy shoe theme. Virginia's so vibrant, inspiring, and alive!"

Older, vital women are a gift! If we're open to their contributions, we won't cheat ourselves out of these kinds of enriching friendship opportunities.

"Interacting with older women is actually more comfortable for me than with women my age. I like the perspective and the depth of conversation they bring to me," says Liz, 54. "I relish hearing where they've been and where they are now. They provide great learning and wisdom that I see reflected into my own life. I'm single, and so I've had a lot of conversations around feeling alone when you enter your sixties and seventies. They've taught me that how I'll fair has to do with my strong friendships and extended family around me. I have an amazing small village of support and love."

Elizabeth and Pam, both in their mid-thirties, have been best friends since second grade when they lived down the street from each other. Today they love hanging out with Lynn, 55, whom Elizabeth met when she and Lynn were newspaper journalists.

"Lynn makes comments about being old, but our friendship is based on who we are and the common interests we hold. We're kindred spirits and great sounding boards for each other," says Elizabeth, a certified yoga instructor. "Before she relocated to Singapore, we would take walks around the reservoir and go out to lunch and movies. My twenties were such a weird place. Even though I'm very close to my mom, she couldn't relate to what I was going through. I relied on Lynn, who's married with two children, to provide counsel and perspective. She's a straight shooter."

When Elizabeth dated a guy no one liked, Lynn was the one who questioned if he was really right for her. Months later Lynn helped Elizabeth meet a man at a fund-raiser. They're now married, with their first child.

"To me, a friend is someone who tells me the truth, inspires me, and is someone I can emulate," says Elizabeth. "Lynn is one of those women."

When considering the twenty-plus-year age gap in their friendship, Lynn says, "I'm age blind. Being around people of different ages gets my head out of *my* problems. I don't want to be like the women who think it sucks to turn forty or fifty. I want to hang out with people who are interested and interesting and who want to expand their horizons."

Spending time with younger women encourages Pat, 64, to try new things. She feels fortunate to belong to a book club with women twenty years her junior.

"I enjoy hearing what the younger women are going through and learning their perspectives. They make me feel connected and encourage me to try new things," says Pat. "It's great to laugh and be carefree for an evening. My mother taught me that age doesn't have anything to do with who we are. She always made sure she had great interests and was doing wonderful things. Because of that she was never a drag, no matter what her age. Mom was a great role model."

Our Friends Fill Us Up in Different Ways

With a wide array of friends, we can turn to different friends for different reasons. What each woman needs and gives varies with culture, background, family status, age, and personality. The GOTCHA! Moment in Chapter 1 suggests picturing a "circle of friends" supporting us throughout life. This visualization may suggest that it's time to think about diversifying our friendships. Perhaps someone we only depend on for certain insights could provide more if we opened up to her in a new way. Or maybe a friend we only invite to do specific things could be included in other activities. Our "circle of friends" may reveal holes filled only by opening our hearts to a variety of women and intentionally bringing them into our lives.

At age sixty, Lael, a self-proclaimed "world hopper," moved from California to Wyoming. In 1993, she knew no one in her small town. Today Lael is an active member in four women's groups. She has built a deep and wide network of women ranging from their twenties to seventies, who all contribute to her life in different and significant ways.

"I'm pretty sure at 79, I am the oldest of any of the groups," says Lael, who, with her husband, recently relocated to the nearby "big city" of Cody yet keeps her connections in both towns. "Ida from Bunko is six months younger than I am—and can you believe we both lived in San Diego County a thousand miles away from here all those years ago?"

So how does someone create such strong, lasting relationships with a variety of friends?

"This is a part of the country where almost everyone is from somewhere else, so, in that way, it makes it easy to reach out," says Lael. "Months after we moved here, I met a woman who had relocated from Colorado, and her husband, an oil guy, was gone a month and home a month. She decided to start a bunco group and invite a bunch of women for her to meet. Today it's like a sorority. We range in age from thirty to, well, me! We catch up with who's doing what, who got divorced, who's getting married, who's a grandmother, or who's working when," says Lael. "There's a dozen of us, so we each only have to host once a year. That means providing the dinner and prizes. There's a show-off thing about who can create the best prizes within a sixty-dollar budget. We have a waiting list of women wanting to get in and a long list of subs. It's like the hub of our community and the peak of our existence. We're a support system; someone is always close by."

If that's not enough, once a month Lael convenes the local Ya-Ya Sisters to eat out at a restaurant or to enjoy a potluck at one of their homes.

"Today there are eight of us, ranging from age sixty-two to me! There are liberals and conservatives, and we discuss world problems. This is not about charity work or drinking wine. We are here to straighten the world out!" Lael muses. "It's totally different from the bunco group."

And the Ya-Yas differ from The Babes, five women ranging from their fifties to, you guessed it, Lael. The Babes focus on social events, such as inviting "orphans" who have no family in town for Thanksgiving dinner. Lael and her husband, Lyle, host an annual New Year's Eve event for some thirty-five Babes and their friends and host a Kentucky Derby party that attracts sixty to seventy people. Please don't confuse The Babes with The Lunch Bunch, six different women Lael meets the second Tuesday of the month.

Since Lael is a born GOTCHA! organizer (see Chapter 8), we asked her how to successfully form or join a group of women committed to Grow Old Together with Courage, Health, and Attitude. According to Lael, give the group a name; calling it something makes it concrete. Then do your part to contribute.

"Once in a group you can't be a blob," says Lael. "To be accepted, have a project or an interest women can connect to—be it a craft, hiking, something you're studying, or raising your kids. Don't sit around and complain; have some sort of purpose. And when you're new to a group, don't talk too much about yourself. Participate quietly; don't be overly pushy. Then ask someone in the group you connect with to go out to lunch or do something, and get to know her better so you have even more of a connection at the next function."

What makes our friends special are their qualities, values, motivations, and interests that add to our lives. Once we know what we want in a friend, it's easier to see beyond differences and discover similarities. We then open ourselves up, not only to new friendships, but to new potential.

Chapter 5

Shake It Up, Mix It Up!
Things to Do to Break Out of That Rut

Friendships, like any relationship, can become stale if we don't shake things up. Variety definitely adds spice to the time we share with our female friends. If the things we do with our friends have grown a little too comfortable and predictable, it's time to break out of the rut.

Women want ideas for what to do with their friends. They long to have memorable experiences. While getting together for coffee or lunch is wonderful, and we don't take that effort for granted, women expressed a desire for more. What else could we do that is exciting and different? How can we mix things up and add some "wow factor" to our girlfriend get-togethers? The commitment it takes to leave the house or office is huge but so worth it! Why not go for the gusto? We've gathered ways to mix it up and shake it up!

Walk and Talk

One simple and preferred way women get together is to walk—and talk. It's free, provides time for in-depth conversation, and helps us stay fit and healthy. While most prefer to be outside in the fresh air, walking at an indoor shopping mall or on a gym track is a fine alternative, as long as we're moving!

Deborah, 45, a corporate trainer, wanted more time with her friends, so she makes it a habit of meeting girlfriends for walk-and-talk dates, both one-on-one and in small groups.

"Combining moving muscles with connecting at the heart feeds my body, mind, and soul," she says.

Christin, 46, a high school special education teacher and breast cancer survivor, was training for a two-day breast cancer walk. She sent out an e-mail inviting friends to gather at her home on Saturday mornings and Sunday afternoons for a one-hour twenty-minute walk. What a great way for women to meet each other, fit in their exercise, and support an important cause! And Christin's preparation with friends paid off. During the two-day walk, she logged 27.7 miles!

Likewise, Lisa, 51, a professional business speaker from Atlanta, Georgia, walks two to three miles twice a week with a friend, regardless of the weather. "Don't walks go quickly when we have someone to talk to?" she asks. "Exercise is easy with a buddy."

Making a walk date is simple. A few text messages, e-mails, or voice messages to confirm the time and place, and it's done. No need for reservations or money. All that's required are good-fitting shoes and a knack for conversation!

Use the time to explore. Take a walking tour of the city, parks, or museums. If you've got a zoo nearby, become "two" with nature. The sights and sounds are incredible. Of course there's nothing like walking on the beach, around a lake, or on a mountain trail to simultaneously experience peace and exhilaration.

Outdoor Activities and Other Adventures

The feeling that we're doing something good for our bodies, minds, and spirits makes engaging in outdoor activities a good choice for girl time. Whether it's jogging, kayaking, hiking, or snow skiing, getting outside and moving with friends is stimulating.

"My friend Michelle and I have been friends for eight years," says Patty, 48. "We've spent time together talking about our sons over coffee, discussing work while consuming 500-calorie lunches, and going nightclubbing when she was single again and I was not. Once tired of that, I suggested she take up golf. That way we could be together while getting some exercise. It was a great way to get a workout and for her to meet men. At the driving range, we'd hit a few balls and then stop and chat. To me, this special time is more refreshing than having lunch or a cocktail."

Each year, DeeDee, 42, meets her two best friends from college for an outdoor adventure. She loves how invigorating it is for her personally and for their friendship.

"One winter we decided to take a cross-country ski trip," she says. "Both of my friends are adventurists, and I'm not. They push me to do things I'd never do on my own. We stayed in rustic cabins at a beautiful mountain resort and spent our days skiing on risky, ungroomed trails on the side of a mountain—not on the safe, flat, groomed paths. I'm cautious, but going beyond my norm unleashed a wide range of emotions; it made me feel great. When I got so caught up in the fun, I had the flickering thought, 'I wish I married someone who did these kinds of things.' Then I realized that my husband can't be everything. That's exactly why these women are in my life. Of course the best part of the trip was the three-hour conversations while we skied, covering everything from work to kids to marriage. We completely 'get' each other and treat each other so well. I can't imagine my life without them."

Lynn, 52, CEO of a health-care ad agency, began playing tennis at age forty. "I had moved out of the city and joined a beach and tennis club," she says. "I started taking lessons and signed up to play on a USTA (United States Tennis Association) league, something I'd never done. I really enjoyed meeting interesting women, many who were working women like me. After a match I'd invite one or two women to my place for a bite to eat. It was a great way to meet friends with similar interests."

As a leadership and relationship expert, Sylvia Lafair, Ph.D., author of *Don't Take It to Work*, is a big proponent of what she calls "outer nature reflection of our inner nature." Rather than engaging in competitive sports, she prefers going on a camping weekend—without the men.

"Being in nature is so critically important for our health and relationships," she says. "Sitting around a campfire under the stars telling stories is very primal. What I've found through work I've done with leadership groups is that, while we might start at one level, just being in the quiet of nature allows us to go deeper. It takes understanding the art of listening versus problem-solving, but when we can give each other that gift, we come away in a beautiful space."

If camping doesn't do it for you, try spending an early evening with girlfriends picnicking at the beach or by a mountain stream.

Sylvia asserts that being around water is deeply feminine. "The site and sound of flowing water helps us to think of movement rather than a static state. In nature, where the sights and sounds are dramatic, we get out of our small mindsets and think larger thoughts. The outer beauty helps us see our inner beauty."

"I love the sea breeze and camaraderie of racing sailboats with other women," says Mary, 57, president of a health-care trade association. "On shore everyone helps each other, and we have great fun. Once we're out on the racecourse, we take no prisoners. The emotional highs and lows of competition are energizing. We don't race for money, and this isn't the America's Cup; but we're intense. To me, racing is a time to recharge and connect. The bond our crew has is incredible. When we bring on a new teammate, her personality has to fit. Each of us has to communicate well and know her part. We all have to be in the right place when we are tacking and setting the sails.

"If you want to meet women friends, find something you like to do, and then join other women who are doing it," advises Mary. "You'll not only make friends but also learn from those women. I'm a peacemaker. Whether racing or on the job, I try to get people to work together and not ruffle feathers. I've sailed with other women who are more direct and have grown from them. And I get to spend time with younger women on the crew, which helps me feel younger than I am!"

Feeling Artsy-Crafty?

It's freeing and fun to exercise a different part of your brain and engage with a friend to make something with your hands. Creation stirs a different kind of energy, while completing a project builds a sense of pride and accomplishment.

How about getting together with other women to make jewelry or sew? Joining friends for a potluck and an evening of beading, sewing, or quilt making engages the creative sides of our brains. Even if we don't have the patience for the intricate work, it's fun to be part of the group, enjoy the conversation, and appreciate what others create.

One sweet friends and crafts gathering is when Kate, 52, and her work colleague Dot meet up every six weeks or so. Dot gathers her needlepoint and takes it to Kate's house. Kate grabs her beading supplies, and the two sit on Kate's deck, crafting and watching pelicans soar over the lake as they chat away a Sunday afternoon.

At age nineteen, Margaret began her teaching career in a four-room schoolhouse in Illinois. The local women, ranging from forty to eighty years old, invited Margaret to their quilting bee. Open to new experiences, Margaret joined the group and learned to quilt. She'd sit with them for hours on a Sunday afternoon, quilting, sharing experiences, and suggesting possible solutions for less-than-favorable circumstances.

"I not only had fun but learned a lot from women who were twice to three or even four times older than I was," says Margaret. "I mastered all sorts of crafty skills with a community of women who expressed friendship while engaging in arts and crafts."

Whether it's a friend who owns a kiln and lets you play in clay or two friends who enjoy painting with watercolor, using art as a medium for growing closer is something we can master.

Shopping for Solace and Spice

Ah, shopping! For many of us, retail therapy spells friendship Valhalla. Looking for that perfect outfit, finding a bargain, or just window-shopping for ideas creates a wonderful, womanly bond.

It's like a treasure hunt. We never know what we'll find, and we hope to be delighted by what we do. When we shop with a friend, it allows us to show off our find or get a second opinion. Best of all, it's the companionship—the woman-to-woman time—that spices up our days or nourishes our souls.

"Two women have never had more fun shopping together than my friend Meryl and me," says Shellie, 65. "It doesn't matter where we shop or what we spend, it's the camaraderie of doing it together. Plus Meryl knows if it doesn't look good on her, I'm the one who'll say, 'Take it off!'"

G✺TCHA! MOMENT

What Do You Want to Do?

Here are thirteen ways to mix up and shake up the routine in your girlfriend time:

1. Share summer vacation pictures over brunch.
2. Bargain shop the Saturday morning flea markets.
3. Indulge in "Sex in the City" cosmos and hors d'oeuvres one night.
4. Learn a digital game or "ping-pong, anyone?"
5. Shake your hips in a Hula-Hoop® or salsa dancing lessons.
6. Clean out a closet, weed the garden, hold a garage sale—at your place first then hers.
7. Paint by numbers, or let it all out at a "stitch and bitch" session.

8. Lunch at your place with fine linens and great music.
9. Ask a few neighbors to walk their kids to school with you.
10. Take a vegetarian or ethnic cooking class with boutique wine pairing.
11. Find all the fountains in your city—bring a sketch pad!
12. Head out on a weekend road trip, or tour a foreign city.
13. Make a YouTube video, sober please!

Mixing Up Your Repertoire

Leslie, 37, CEO of a marketing strategy company, is single with no children. After a breakup, and to ensure her business thrived during a recession, she immersed herself in her work, accepting every dinner invitation and networking event she could to meet potential clients. She felt like there were never enough hours in the day, and finally by the end of the year, she felt burned out and exhausted.

"I knew I couldn't keep going at that pace, so I set a time with myself for a reflection session," says Leslie. "I asked myself that important question, 'Years from now, when I look back at my life, what will I say matters?' As much as I love my business and have a passion for it, I knew it was not what was going to make me happy. At that moment I realized how important my friends were to me. They carried me through my breakup, yet I didn't feel that I let them know how much I appreciated them. They were the ones who made me happy; yet I was spending time *in* lots of places, but not time *with* the people I really wanted to be with. So I put spending time with girlfriends in my annual goals. I was very specific that I would spend at least an hour a week with a friend. This would not be in a group setting but one-on-one, focused time either in person or on the phone."

And so, being an organized person, Leslie began to calendar appointments with what she calls her "drop-everything" friends. "If mid-week I realized I had not met my goal, I would call someone I hadn't talked to or seen and set a date to do something," she says. "If I didn't catch her the first time, I'd keep trying."

In addition to setting the weekly goal, Leslie also created a vision for having at least one silly experience. So she reached out to her friend Myla, 37, a single inner-city schoolteacher, and they decided to enter a two-woman team adventure race held an hour away from their homes in Houston, Texas.

"We planned it for months," says Leslie. "The race included biking, rowing, and running. We weren't experts in any of those sports, but we weren't worried about winning, just finishing. We never practiced because we figured we could get through somehow. It was such a laugh. We got to the 1.5-hour race, and they gave us a map and a list of challenges, such as running to point A, biking to point B, and rowing to point C. In between there were surprise challenges. We had our moments, like when Myla crabbed at me, 'You didn't tell me there was this much rowing!' We had never rowed before in our lives.

"When it was time to swim, I went negative and said we didn't need to do that part. But Myla ran off the end of the pier and jumped in, leading the way. I admired her, and I knew I had to follow, even though I didn't bring a change of clothes. It was a metaphor for our friendship. We supported each other during the frustrating moments, and we laughed ourselves silly, like the time we rowed in circles in the middle of the lake.

"After the race, we went out for lunch and sat for hours talking and laughing. Getting out and doing that together made a huge difference in our friendship. While going out to eat or to the movies is nice, doing something so bizarre allowed for a deeper, stronger connection. We had to promise each other that we'd do it again—but not without the other!"

Spa Time

Lolma finds quality time with friends in visiting a day spa. "We get massages, sit in the hot tub, and chat," says the 62 year old. "It's a special place to nurture ourselves and our relationships."

It's at the spa that Lolma says she actually enjoys gossiping. "It's great to talk about who did what for whom and how we felt about it," she muses. "We know what we say is strictly confidential and that we have our friends' best interests in mind. We just need to talk things through sometimes," she says.

Many women we spoke with felt that, because of the intimacy, solace, and healing environment, time at the spa is a perfect girlfriend treat. Diane and Noonie don't need spa treatments to find that kind of soul-quenching respite. They often just pay a small fee at a day spa to sit in the steam room or get side-by-side pedicures. Taking care of ourselves without the distraction of phone calls, texts, or e-mails permits us to relax. It's the complete break from "real" life for a few hours that allows us to breathe deeply and connect with ourselves and our friends. Getting away from the pressures of our to-do lists helps us get in touch with our feelings and emotions. And we can then share them for input and perspective, if we wish. In a spa setting, we recognize the unspoken agreement to be with each other, and nothing else is going to interrupt our time to retreat.

So how else can we get such respite? We all need to disconnect, even if only for a short while. Next time we go someplace soothing, be it the beach or a walk in the hills, let's try detaching from other forms of input. We can tell our family we'll be unreachable, except for emergencies, until a certain hour. Let's claim this time for ourselves, and avoid looking at personal or work e-mails or thinking of all the errands or events awaiting us. Instead, we'll give ourselves permission to just be present and rejuvenate!

Traveling with Girlfriends

Getting away with girlfriends is a major treat, whether it's for a short road trip to see another friend, a hiking adventure, visiting museums in another city, or traveling abroad. While past generations of married women may not have left their husbands for a few days or weeks to travel with a female friend, a number of women we spoke to say their husbands support their travel. And for those women who are single, having girlfriends to travel with is a godsend.

Linda, 53, who has always been single, says that while she has taken vacations on her own and has met nice women and men on tours, she prefers to travel with a good friend.

"Vacationing on my own is OK, but it gets lonely," says Linda. "I find myself telling my life story over and over again. If I vacation with a friend, I don't have to rehash who I am and why I'm traveling solo. Recently, I met two women in their seventies who met through a grief support group and were on a vacation in Ireland. Deciding to travel together, they realized they were destined to meet each other, and their friendship was meant to be. Throughout my entire life, I have always known that men will come and go, but my women friends are my foundation."

Susan, 60, an executive coach, has a twenty-year tradition of meeting her sister (yes, sisters count as friends) at a different spa each year. "We live across the country from each other. We didn't like the fact that when we got to see each other, we were surrounded by our spouses and kids. We missed our alone time. So we started this annual tradition of going to a different warm-weather spa as a winter getaway. I feel really lucky to have this time with her."

In addition to devoting one hour a day to girlfriend time, Leslie, 37, also promised herself to spend at least one weeklong vacation with a friend annually. She had no idea how that goal would manifest itself, but serendipitously she connected with Danielle, a woman she met in the summer of 1992 when traveling in Russia just after the fall of communism.

"We've never lived in the same city, and I'm not even sure we'd like each other if we did, but we're great travel companions," says Leslie. "The last time we traveled together was in 1998 when Danielle joined me on a road trip from Chicago to Houston. One evening years later, when I was feeling sorry for myself after a breakup with my boyfriend, the phone rang. I answered, and when I heard Danielle's voice, I started crying. She said, 'Uh-oh,' and I told her the whole story. When I finished, she announced, 'We're going on a road trip. You need something to look forward to.'"

Danielle invited Leslie to join her in Montana's Glacier National Park for a week. "We rode horses, hiked, and read books," says Leslie. "That year, I relearned how important friends are, especially because I'm single without kids. I had done myself a disservice getting so caught up in my work. I don't want the day-to-dayness of life to get in the way of the people I care about and who nurture me. Without my friends, I'd be lost."

Couple Time

If you share life with a partner, it's always a plus when your partner gets along with your girlfriend's partner. It allows more time with her and a deeper understanding of each other's life. Remember, meeting a new couple can lead to an additional couple as friends and to a new girlfriend as well.

Amanda, 26, met her close friend Brittany in nursing school. Fortunately Amanda's boyfriend, Jeff, and Brittany's husband, Jake, have a lot in common, so it makes it easy for the couples to get along. A few years ago, they moved into the same apartment complex, so sharing time is even easier—as is taking turns pet sitting their sister Goldendoodle dogs!

"Occasionally we go on what we call a 'suburban date,' eating at a local restaurant and going to a movie," says Amanda. "When we're trying to save money, we'll do game night. We go to their place, or they'll come to ours in PJs. We cook dinner, play games, and watch Netflix. We enjoy double dates to the shooting range and theme parks. A few times a year, we go to Jake's parents' home on a lake where we boat, Jet Ski, and lie in hammocks. It's like Disney World for our dogs, Sofia and Lola, and it wears them out! It's so much fun for all of us."

Likewise, Pamela, 34, says that she and her friend, Elizabeth, are fortunate their husbands like each other.

"We call it '*bro*mance!' And since Elizabeth and I value our one-on-one time, we encourage our guys to hang out with one another. The day we went to pick out my wedding dress, my then-fiancé, Travis, went over to Elizabeth's house to help her husband paint their new baby's room. When we got home, the two guys were on the computer and drinking beer. With the guys bonding, it's easy for us to do things as couples. We love to have dinner and play Wii™ as a foursome."

Karen, 52, a dental practice manager and the mother of two grown sons, is married to Robin, a high school football coach. She met Fran and Steve while watching the Friday night football games.

"Week after week we sat next to each other, watched the game, and chatted," says Karen. "When Fran and I discovered that both of us had lost our first husbands, we had an immediate connection. She is someone who completely understands what I'm feeling. With each game and after-game party, we grew closer and closer. Now we spend a lot of time off the football field as couples, from going on weekend walks to renting a house at the beach. In addition to enjoying our time as a foursome, Fran and I love doing girlfriend things. In fact, she called the other day from the gym asking where I was because the class would be more fun if I were there. *That* made me feel awesome."

You may discover that a girlfriend can lead to a couple friendship, or a couple friendship can lead to an unexpected best girlfriend. Whichever way it happens, it's definitely worth going for!

Getting It on the Calendar: Who Decides What When

Talk is cheap. Ideas are great, but to make something happen, someone has got to make a plan and set a time to meet! How do women fit in girl time when the pressures and responsibilities seem all consuming and exhausting?

SUNDAY	MONDAY	TUESDAY	WEDNESDAY	THURSDAY	FRIDAY	SATURDAY
				Split up the to-do's: set time, make reservations, pick the movie, reminder email		
Standing dates						
	Think ahead... send out an email with an idea		Evite...a reason to connect and include		Respond one way or the other	

"I envy women who book things in advance," says Lynn, 52. "Typically it's Friday evening and I'm hanging out with my husband, thinking I should have made plans to see friends over the weekend! I don't like spending a lot of time on the phone, but I will make a quick call to my girlfriends to see who's free to do something. Standing dates help, like the weekend morning walks I take with Darlene and the every-two-month dinner I have with a group of longtime friends."

"With all the attention we have to give our children, spouses, and aging parents, it's crucial to plan ahead," says Marie, 50. "It takes time and coordination, but the reward is huge. We always end up asking, 'Why didn't we do this sooner?'"

According to Marie, it's vital that we not keep score of who plans what when. "Someone has to take the lead to make the dinner reservation, book the flight, or decide where to meet, and I don't mind being that person," she says. "If you want to have fun and companionship, I suggest *just do it!*"

When finding something to do and a friend to do it with, Sidonie, 51, who works in homeland security, likes to think of it as slicing up a pie. "Inventory the interests in your life," she suggests. "I like spending free time at museums, seeing movies, going to the farmers' market, and dragging a friend through a craft fair now and then. I have to find someone who fits that slice of the pie and then ask her to join me in the adventure."

Life can be an adventure, so get out, and enjoy it even more with a friend!

The Journey, Not the Destination, Matters Most

If you and your friends are still stumped by what to do when you're together, remember, it's not just about what you *do* it's about what you *give* and *receive* in the *doing*. The richness of the connection—the back-and-forth exchange—is what's important.

"Women are relationship people," says Sylvia Lafair, Ph.D., a leadership education and relationship expert. "Rarely do two women call each other and ask, 'How about those Broncos?' For us, it's about the subtleties of relationships. We can listen to each other without judgment and say, 'Here's another way of looking at it.' We can share perceptions without the attachment of 'I want you to do what I think is best.' By doing so, we give our friends the room to find their own answers."

"Sisterfriends" is the word Demetra Gayle, 62, uses to describe the women who are sharing life's journey at her side. Though they have no biological connection, Demetra Gayle, Colette, and Taj have ties that bind. For ten years they belonged to a community meeting for African-

American Healers, and even though the group has disbanded, the three "sisterfriends" are bonded for life!

"They are there for me, and I'm there for them no matter what!" explains Demetra Gayle, a full-time adornments artist and retired psychotherapist/social worker. "We're as close as some blood-related sisters—and probably closer than many who grew up in the same family."

What's the difference between friends and "sisterfriends"? According to Demetra Gayle, it's the level of commitment. It's even in the way they spell the word: "sisterfriends" vs. sister-friends. It's *that* connected.

"When one of us gets really sick or is in need, we don't just say, 'I hope you feel better,' we go and stay until they do," she says. "When Taj's sixteen-year-old daughter passed in a tragic accident, I spent the night with her and her ex-husband," says Demetra Gayle. "We've been through deaths, births, breakups, and adventures.

"We support each other's dreams," she continues. "When I went to Europe to attend a four-month leather school, Taj traveled to stay with me for three weeks. She walked with me to the monastery where my classes were held, had coffee with me at a local café, and was there for dinner when I came home."

Similarly Demetra Gayle supports Colette, who is currently in the throes of rewriting her novel. "Sometimes I will just go over to her place and have a sleepover. I do my thing, and she does hers. We just spend time together. I may be knitting something or sewing some leather thing, and she'll be writing on her computer. At my wedding earlier this year, both had a big role in the ceremony, and both were right there to help me dress and get ready."

"Sisterfriends" can talk about anything. "We aren't afraid to say, 'I need an unenlightened moment or an endarkenment day!'" says Demetra Gayle. "That's when you need to talk really badly about someone who has done something terrible, or when one of us has been really hurt by someone, or when we just have those little vicious moments when we want to talk badly about a woman's choice of shoes or lipstick—we don't do that often, honest! We all strive to live out loud, with honesty and integrity, and with a commitment to community service and connection—and realness."

Hanging out may be what "sisterfriends" do best. Imagine no agenda, no deadlines, no reservations, and no preconceived notion, except to be there for each other—mind, body, and spirit! What a refreshing way to share time.

Whether sharing frivolous pastimes, engaging in intense conversations, or just being by each other's side to offer moral support, what women want most is to really be *with* their friends—whatever they're doing. Sometimes, however, shifts in our lives mean that our friends are not as available to do the things we love to do together. Janelle says her thirties are an interesting time and require her to accept new realities.

"It seems like my friends are either having babies or splitting up," says Janelle. "I'm married with no children yet, and while I know how wonderful and life changing babies can be, I can feel a little on the outside. So I am working to keep my expectations of my friends in check. In between seeing them, I am engaging in hobbies like taking piano lessons and traveling with my husband. Plus I know when I do have a baby, I'll get great advice and their maternity clothes!"

When we're with our friends, we can savor the moments by truly being *with* them, not just physically but mentally as well. If we've ever found ourselves halfheartedly paying attention to our girlfriends because we're multitasking or letting our minds wander, we might want to follow one young woman's lead.

Kelley, 24, is working to pay closer attention to her friends when they're talking, just as she and her husband, Chris, are trying to do.

"We discovered that when one of us is talking, if the other person is doing something else while listening to us, it signals that our relationship is not as important as the task at hand," she says. "It's hard, but we try to turn the laptop the other way or put the TV on mute and look at each other during the whole conversation. It makes the person who's talking feel much more valued, avoids miscommunications, and reminds us that our relationship is more important than things and tasks. I am now trying to use this same technique with my girlfriends."

Lolma recalls really being there with her friend Deena while they sat on a park bench. "It was one of those moments you know you'll remember forever. Deena had malignant cancer. We knew we would not be with each other much longer. We were fully present and right in the moment. I try to be like that with all my friends, to really *get* that this is precious time and treat it like it won't ever happen again."

Paying attention to our friends and the nuances of their lives deepens friendships. The laughter and tears, the tense moments and funny incidents, and the scheming and dreaming bring us closer. It's these fond memories and good feelings that make us want to get together again and again! In other words, who wouldn't want to spend time with women we want to grow old with?

Chapter 6

Virtual Friends: Not Letting Distance Deter Us

Though it may take extra effort, fanning the flames of friendship is possible when time zones and geography separate us. We don't have to let a friend who lives miles away fade from the forefront of our lives just because we're not getting as much face time as we might crave. What really matters is staying connected and avoiding emotional distance that compounds the physical separation.

With social and digital media, it's easier than ever to remain part of each other's life. Even if we use the tried-and-true phone or postal service, we demonstrate interest in our friend's life and well-being. Being there in spirit during those critical moments, when a friend's understanding and support matter most, further cements our friendships.

Reach Out to Stay Connected

Many women shared that maintaining and growing long-distance relationships is challenging. Lois, a 73-year-old therapist and energy worker, confesses, "I would say this is one of my weaknesses. I think I'm pretty good at keeping the relationship alive with people who make the effort. I'm just not the initiator."

Consistently staying connected is the foundation of thriving long-distance friendships. That might entail setting a time to talk each week, posting regularly on her Facebook wall, arranging a weekend getaway, or buying a webcam so you can see each other now and then.

"We're so lucky to live in these times," says Deborah, 48. "My parents left Ireland in the 1960s, and it cost a fortune for them to stay in touch with family and friends. Today we're blessed with technology. Since more than half my family is in Ireland, I communicate with quick e-mails or an update on Facebook when I get up in the morning. It only takes a few minutes to check in or reach out. If I have a long commute, I use that time to call friends I don't see very often. When I travel and I'm in an area where I have friends, I'll stay an extra night just to visit with them."

Liz, 54, uses e-mail to keep in touch with her friend Liza, who lives on the opposite coast. "One evening I was looking for an hors d'oeuvres recipe, and I e-mailed her to send it to me. I didn't hear back for a few days, which is on the edge of our response time. So I picked up the phone and left a message to make sure she was OK. Sure enough, that night I got an e-mail with a link to her photo-share site with thirty of her latest fabulous photos. I knew immediately she was all right and was confident that in the next few weeks, we'd call and talk for hours."

Susan and Linda live thousands of miles away. They use voice mail to the extreme to keep in touch with each other's life. It all began with using the voice mail system when they both worked at a large technology company. After they left the company, they found an independent, password-protected voice mail system to support this communication style. For the past twenty years, they've left messages without calling each other's phone.

"We have the voice mail number on speed dial and send each other up to ten voice mails a day," says Susan. "I'll call and leave Linda a message; then she'll listen when it's convenient and comment on my message. It's just part of my routine. I get up in the morning, read the paper, and pick up my voice mails from Linda. She doesn't sleep well, so on any given night, she may leave me two to three messages. I think our system works so well because Linda is much more talkative than I am. I tend to lose myself in other people. This way I don't have to fight for time, and I know Linda is listening to me."

Susan continues, "We can say anything to each other any time of the day. It's like a personal journal I share with a friend. I almost can't put it into words. It helps relieve that universal feeling of being alone. Linda and I share in each other's joys and fears. We bounce ideas off each other. I know I have someone who will listen to me and support me, no matter what's going on.

"After I was diagnosed with breast cancer, if I woke up with a night terror, I'd call our voice mail system, knowing I could leave a message in a safe place. It's like having a therapist on call. We know we always have each other's best interest at heart. There's nothing that could take me out of my relationship with Linda. That's a really huge safety net. She will always be someone who has my back, but more than that, she is someone who has walked with me through my life journey."

Even though they may only meet physically a few times a year, Susan and Linda are always part of each other's life. It's their system and their discipline implementing it that allow for a rich and lengthy friendship.

Ellen, 60, has been friends with Mary since they met in summer camp at age ten. They live far apart and haven't seen each other for ten years, but they talk, laugh, and cry as if they were in each other's living room.

"We e-mail all the time," says Ellen. "When she doesn't call for a while, I know she's really depressed. I don't press it because I know she'll call when she's ready. We have the good fortune to pick up where we left off and not require an apology. It's like we never missed a beat. That's a testament to the kind of friendship that transcends time and circumstances. It's so important that we treat our friends well because we never know when we'll need them. The deeper the friendship, the more timeless, unconditional, and authentic it is, whether you live across the street or across the country."

We may not have friendships that are decades long. Perhaps our dearest friend passed away. Maybe we had a falling out with a close confidant. We don't have to let the past negatively impact our future. Staying connected with new friends allows those friendships to deepen and evolve. Putting in the effort to reach out, whether it's virtually or eyeball to eyeball, will provide fodder for significant and satisfying relationships. Don't let opportunities to keep connected slip away. It takes real effort to have an enduring and lasting friendship.

G✳TCHA! MOMENT

Sharing a Virtual Glass of Wine

Busy people attract busy people. Hectic schedules get in the way if we indulge in "She's not calling me because she doesn't want to be my friend" talk. Have some compassion for yourself and others. Get creative about the ways you can be together! Think outrageous. Be unreasonable. Here are half a dozen ideas for starters:

1. Set a time via e-mail or text to have a glass of wine together—virtually. Then sip and chat just like you would if your friend were next to you.
2. Dream about a getaway together. Send Internet links to places the two of you can visit. Set a time to talk about them, and make plans!
3. Enjoy a virtual walk and talk on your cell phones. Keep each other company, and share the interesting things you're seeing in your neck of the woods.
4. Start a chain letter by mail or e-mail. Add just a sentence or several paragraphs each time you get it. After a year look back at your rantings, ravings, and adventures.
5. Play a rousing game of Scrabble online. Perhaps include a few friends in this virtual gathering.

6. Send postcards to let your friend know you're think-
    ing of her. When you visit someplace you know she'd
    love, suggest you go back there together.

Face Time Matters

With all the social networking tools available, hearing a friend's
voice, seeing her face, or sharing a hug and a meal still trumps the virtual
world for many women.

"Technology is a great way to stay in touch or to find a friend from
second grade," says Pamela, 34, a corporate attorney. "But I don't want
to solely rely on e-mail. I can say in a few minutes what might take five
pages or more in e-mail. Similarly, Facebook is a nice way to meet people
and to connect, but I won't use it to maintain a friendship. One-on-one
time matters more."

Pamela says that she and her best friend, Elizabeth, keep in touch
constantly. Elizabeth calls Pamela every night on her drive home from
work, but even that doesn't take the place of face-to-face contact.

"If for some reason I go a few days without seeing Elizabeth, I feel
out of sorts," says Pamela. "I like to look into her eyes and know she's
really listening and understanding what I'm saying. We've been friends
since elementary school, so she knows when I want feedback and when
I'm just venting. I never need to explain or worry that she's judging me.
It's so valuable to have someone so close because I can skip over things
and just say something like, 'You need to talk me off the ledge,' and she
completely gets what I'm saying and what I need."

Getting together is also critical to Molly, 58, a business owner, who
became friends with Julie thirty-five years ago when they worked in a
restaurant. Julie moved to Portland, Oregon, a two-hour plane ride away
from Molly's home in Northern California. She flies back annually to
celebrate her birthday with Molly and other friends.

For Julie's fortieth birthday, Molly surprised her and turned the tables by flying to Portland. "I had planned it all out with her husband," says Molly. "One Saturday, I just showed up in her bathroom when she was fixing her hair and still in her pajamas. Shocked, Julie hugged me and squealed. I told her to get dressed because a tour guide was picking us up and taking us to the Columbia River Gorge, where we'd picnic and drink wine. 'I don't care if we just drive around the block for the rest of the day!' she exclaimed. What a special weekend."

When both women lost their mothers within a six-month period, they designed a weekend away in Scottsdale, Arizona, to comfort each other.

"I brought some wonderful books on grief and meditation that we read daily," says Molly. "While Julie leans toward Buddhism and I was raised Catholic, we share the same spiritual belief that there's something bigger and better, and it doesn't matter what we each call it. We both are authentic, kind, and honest with a strong set of morals for how we conduct ourselves. We wanted to walk through our loss with a sense of grace and dignity, and we knew we needed to lean on each other for support."

Nalini lives in India and her dearest friend, Jette, resides in Switzerland. The two, both in mid-life, met at a women's luncheon in Pune, India, when their husbands were attending a nuclear physics meeting.

"It was a regular ladies luncheon, a group that met every two weeks," remembers Nalini. "A new face was unusual, particularly when it was a foreigner. Jette, who is Danish, sat to the side, not looking very comfortable, bundled up in a sari.

"When I spoke to her, I understood the reason for her discomfort. She had been forced to put on a sari that belonged to her host over her jeans and T-shirt so she would fit in better! She was visiting with her husband who had an assignment in Pune, and she was at loose ends. I invited her over to my home and took her shopping and sightseeing. I didn't think I would see her once she left; travel out of India is not very easy.

"When I happened to go to Europe, she invited me to visit, and that first chance meeting was the beginning of an enduring thirty-five-year-old friendship. Obviously we share something, because we were once in Copenhagen, Denmark, and a Turkish store owner asked if we were sisters! That was so bizarre because she is blonde with fair skin, and I have brown skin and dark hair! There's nothing in our appearance that would make us seem related, but he saw our commonality. We are alike in so many ways!"

Nalini and Jette visit in person at least twice a year and, in between, stay connected by phone.

"It's almost better to have your best friend not live in the same city so that you can share confidences you might not otherwise," Nalini says. "I trust Jette completely. I accept her advice because she knows my family and me so well, even though we live so far apart. And I think it's the same for her.

"Through the years my family has come to accept that I have close friends I'll travel to visit or have visit me," says Nalini. "In India men can be quite controlling and expect women to put aside things that are important to them. My husband has come to respect that this is important to me. My family now understands this is something I have to do. I'm fortunate I have the means to travel. The older I get, the more I understand the value of real friendship!"

Nalini shared this story of enduring friendship with Diane on a flight from San Francisco to New York. On her way home to India, Nalini instantly related to this global topic of intentional women friendships. A year later Nalini reached out to Diane to let her know that she would be in San Francisco celebrating the birth of her grandson. The two made plans to rendezvous and explore their initial interest in each other and the possibility of an intriguing long-distance friendship.

Nalini's expression of unreasonableness in friendship is inspiring! While we might easily explain away our hesitation to travel thousands of miles "just to see a friend," breaking loose of the habits that keep us stuck in our everyday routines makes the extraordinary possible. Defending and justifying our existing lifestyles don't allow for new and compelling futures with women we want to grow old with.

Be There for Important Milestones

Taking part in people's lives is what makes for enduring friendships—remembering a birthday or anniversary, and acknowledging a promotion or the passing of a loved one. Reaching out during an illness or providing encouragement during a family trauma communicates an immediate "you matter to me" message.

While there are always a million reasons not to take the time or effort, there are certain milestones in friends' lives when putting all else aside *really* matters. Don't we remember who stood by our side when we moved through certain passages of life? While other obligations distract us, there's something magical about the friend who goes out of her way to be at a son's bar mitzvah, husband's deployment, or child's wedding. It takes effort, but the women who actually show up in our lives are the ones we count as true friends. And if you can't be there in person, send a note or a token to show that you're there in spirit. Set up structures to support you in remembering. Write a sticky note, put it in your calendar, send yourself an e-mail, or ask a friend to remind you. It's that important! Don't let these milestones go unnoticed or unrecognized.

Reinvigorating Long-Distance Relationships

It's never too late! Reconnecting with women who once played an important part in our lives can lead to renewed and enduring relationships. Most women respond with surprise and delight when a former friend reaches out to rekindle a friendship. That's what Leesa, 53, a legal marketer, found when she got back in touch with her college friends.

"Sometime between my thirties and forties, I lost touch with these special women," she says. "We all live in different parts of the country, so I went through our college alumni association to find them. One of these special women was my old college roommate, Kim. I hadn't spoken to her in twenty years. I wasn't sure what her reaction would be when she received the e-mail request from the association, but I figured I had nothing to lose by getting back in touch. Kim did connect with me, and I learned she lived in Southern California. In 2008, when I had a conference in Los Angeles, I contacted her for brunch. We were like two old college buds. Our relationship hadn't changed a bit. It was such a special feeling because friends like her are part of the fabric of my life. There are times when we are not as close, but it can come back full circle when we reconnect and find common ground."

Because Leesa's communication with her long-distance friends is primarily virtual, she does little things to bridge the gap. "I'll send them a short e-mail, an electronic card, a link to an article I know will interest them, or give them a phone call to tell them I'm thinking of them," she says. "It takes energy and time, and I'm not the world's greatest at it. Sometimes a week or two goes by before I get back to someone, but keeping in touch is very fulfilling and rewarding. It makes my life so much richer."

When Leesa travels, she makes a point to let her friends know she'll be in town. She arrives early or stays late to be with them. "That keeps the connections alive with people who mean so much to me," she says. "Recently I learned that my friend from Chicago, Illinois, was coming into town. I sent her an e-mail and invited her to dinner. She responded with, 'You made my day!' It took half a minute, and she was ecstatic. We met for dinner, and during that time, we discussed an upcoming meeting for a nonprofit board we both serve on. We decided to meet in Denver, Colorado, ahead of time for a spa weekend. How great that we stayed in touch!"

Lynn, 55, a journalist, recently relocated to Singapore from the United States. The move made her think about friendships and the women she was leaving. "A house is a house, but friendships in a community are really hard to leave," says Lynn. "I know it will be up to me to stay in touch, but the sixteen-hour time difference will make it even more challenging. I'll have to be proactive and intentional about it."

To keep connected, she and four friends from Northern California get together virtually. "They Skype me every week, which lets me see and hear them," says Lynn. "While they're having wine and appetizers on a Thursday evening, I'm having Friday-morning orange juice. It means so much to me. When we see each other in person once or twice a year, the conversation just continues. This takes it from the usual, 'So how's Singapore?' that I get from most people to being much more specific and in the moment, such as, 'So how was the party you went to last weekend and was that strange woman drunk as usual?'"

G✸TCHA! MOMENT

What's Stopping You from Reconnecting?

If hearing about women who've stayed connected over decades or repaired estranged friendships is more depressing than inspirational, you're not alone. While you may long for rewarding friendship histories, getting there often demands time, energy, a little tongue biting, or some pride swallowing. You may have to admit that you had to put a relationship on hold due to circumstances. You might have to explain that you now have the desire and resources to dedicate to the friendship. No matter what you say or how you say it, rejection or indifference is a possibility. Remember, you can't lose what you haven't tried to win. Try listing the worst thing that could possibly happen if you reach out to a long-lost friend, and she doesn't reciprocate. What feelings would be there for you?

_____

_____

_____

_____

_____

_____

Now take a moment to put on paper how you would handle such rejection. You could say:

- ❄ I appreciate your feelings. I'd really like you to think about what I said.
- ❄ You're right that a lot has happened between then and now. I'm hoping to move on with the same passion and compassion we had before, discovering new ways to connect.
- ❄ Thank you for your honesty; if you reconsider, I am here.

Remember, your friend wasn't anticipating your outreach. She may be surprised or feeling guilty for letting the friendship dissolve. Be generous with your words and thoughts. In the meantime, put your energy into someone near you who's receptive to your efforts.

Maintaining a long-distance relationship requires that *both* women engage. If we feel the friendship becoming one-sided, it's time for authentic communication. Lasting friendships don't happen accidentally. When we have the courage to say what we want and stand for fulfilling and satisfying relationships, miracles happen.

Being conscious of the rewards in reaching out and nurturing friendships will keep us in action, if not immediately, then eventually. Taking risk is the access to the next level of fulfillment. Compassion for ourselves and others is a guideline for having "women you want to grow old with" become a flourishing reality.

Chapter 7

Breakdowns, Pitfalls, and Restoring Balance

Friends can tick us off, just like family. And since we have no blood ties or holidays when we *have* to see them, it's easier to write off friends than relatives. But does this really make sense? Working through relationship issues with a girlfriend is not always easy. Nevertheless, it's the key to an enduring and meaningful friendship.

Whenever we authentically let someone into our lives, we become vulnerable. The more we reveal who we really are, the more sensitive we are when someone says or does something that touches a nerve and reactivates strong feelings and emotions.

It's naive to think that "real" friends never have upsets or breakdowns in their relationships. After all, isn't a *true* friend always there for us? Don't *loyal* friends find ways to kiss and make up? Doesn't a *real* friend say and do the right thing? All the time?

These kinds of "myths" about friendship can permeate our thinking, impact our behavior, and thwart budding or even fully blossomed friendships. Don't buy into the myth, "*True* friends are always aligned, forever supportive, and fully enthusiastic about me and my life." Real friends sometimes hurt each other, sometimes are unthinking, and sometimes display selfish behavior and judgmental attitudes. Powerfully dealing with and overcoming these momentary upsets is the mortar between the building blocks of friendship. Don't we know that when we successfully work through a breakdown, it can strengthen the friendship bond? The commitment to the relationship can be expressed and renewed in a way that wasn't possible in the everyday routine of the friendship.

We've spoken to women who say that even though they consider themselves as close as sisters with certain friends, there are times when they fight like cats and dogs.

"Sometimes we're so close to a girlfriend that we can get on each other's nerves and have it out, but then twenty minutes later we're deciding where to go have lunch," says Rochelle, 47, a massage therapist. "When we let it all out with our friends, feelings do get hurt. But regardless of what might have been said, we know we can always count on one another, and we always have each other's back."

Yet Rochelle has another friend with whom she never shares a cross word. She's known Sharon since their sons were born twenty-five years ago. While a three-hour time difference separates them, they talk several times a day. Sometimes they even watch a TV show together, and when one says she's getting something to drink, the other follows suit.

"We just don't fight," says Rochelle. "If we don't agree with one another, we say so, move on, and then let it go."

Even though Rochelle handles conflicts differently in her friendships, she always works through issues with openness and honesty. Whether vehemently disagreeing or calmly expressing differences, the important thing is that the issue at hand does not stop the friendship. The commitment to the relationship remains stable, regardless of the personalities and styles.

Many women work through disagreements and disappointments with transparency, integrity, respect, and no judgment.

"My friend Brittany and I occasionally travel together, and we know that we can only hang out so long before quirky things about the other person will start annoying us," says Amanda, 26. "Sometimes we'll just say, 'You're stressing me out,' or 'You're driving me nuts.' When too many of those kinds of comments come up, we have to confess that we're sorry and just tired and getting snappy. We have moved beyond the superficial in our friendship, knowing that we will not always be happy and that sometimes we will have wished the other had not said something."

Friends want friends who will tell them what they *really* think and feel, not just what they *want* to hear. Of course we need to take into account our friend's personality and serve things up in a way we know she'll listen best.

Patty, 48, and her friend Debra had been very close friends for more than eight years. But when Patty chaired an art auction for their sons' school and Debra served on the committee, they had an almost-fatal friendship breakdown.

"One of the things that got us in trouble was text messaging," says Patty. "I like to be short and direct. Debra, who is a therapist and more analytical, sent long messages that I found confusing. I would just respond, 'We'll discuss tomorrow,' because I knew I would be seeing her. That frustrated Debra, and she told my son, 'Tell your mom we need to set up a play date because she won't respond.' Not confronting me directly really upset me. Since we were both emotionally ramped up, we agreed to table the issue until after the auction. Three weeks later we met. For me, nothing had changed in our relationship, but not so for Debra. She let me have it and with both barrels. Then we both gave each other feedback that revealed some blind spots. We saw that we each had expectations that weren't stated out loud. Eventually we worked things out, and because we valued each other, we healed and grew as friends. Today we are closer than ever! We really did heal with time."

It's the mythical thinking of what friends "should" be like that limits or even permanently damages our relationships. In revealing and dispelling these "shoulds," we can analyze what actually happened, admit the role we played, and recommit to growing the friendship.

Choosing Who We Let into Our Lives

As in any partnership, how we get along with our friend depends on the personalities involved. Each person's values, family dynamics, culture, and needs play a huge part in how we'll react in times of stress.

And if we're friends with someone long enough, at some point we'll hit a snag in the relationship. While we no doubt realize that everything can't always be perfect, being mindful of the issues that come between us will up the odds of compatibility.

"For me, it's important to identify the friends with whom I want a stronger relationship and to work really hard on those," says Liz, 54. "My friend Maggie is a pivotal friendship I would never want to lose. Years ago, when discussing family matters while sitting on her front porch, she noted, 'You piss me off. Telling me what to do drives me crazy!' Clear about how much Maggie means to me, I solidly said, 'I know, I know; I'll listen. Thanks for telling me. I care about you, and I want to know when I'm bugging you.'

"I feel that deliberately stating and acting on intentions is critical," continues Liz. "So the next time Maggie came over to my house to download things, I didn't try to solve her problem. I played my role of listening and supporting her. It has been twenty-five years since this first incident. I'm not perfect, and I have certainly jumped in many times forgetting to listen…but she reminds me of my habit, and we move forward."

It's critical to balance the positive aspects of a friendship with the more challenging ones. Getting clear about what we're *not* willing to dance with allows us to authentically communicate what works and what doesn't. While we can let certain things slide, *putting up* with personality traits is very different from *compromising* our needs and values for the sake of the friendship.

Friends help shape who we are and how we see the world. Our lives are greatly affected by the people with whom we associate. Friends contribute to our attitudes, outlooks, and choices. Let's be careful to pick friends who add to, not detract from, our lives. It can be hard to have a positive, can-do attitude day in and day out, but why complicate things with friends who make our lives harder or darker?

We have a choice in friendship. We *can* move away from those who negatively impact us and toward those who bring the energy we want or need. We can keep relationships strong by successfully overcoming friendship pitfalls and dealing powerfully with the breakdowns that are inevitable in close relationships.

Seven Deadly Friendship Pitfalls

There will always be friendship breakdowns and pitfalls. When we fall into one, it's essential to recognize where we've landed, take quick action to get out, and move on.

1. **Pretending Nothing's Wrong.** Let's not be scared to say what we think and feel. When something's bothering us, it's best to engage truthfully and get "it" on the table. We shouldn't sell ourselves or our friends short by glossing things over or pretending nothing's wrong. If we're thoughtful in our delivery and come from our hearts, we'll attack the issue not our friend. Sandye, 53, sometimes responds with a simple, straightforward "That's not very nice," "Stop that," or "Don't do that anymore." Since it's not in her nature to hurt people's feelings, this quick "out" allows her and her friends to move on and not dwell on something she finds upsetting.

2. **Taking Things Personally.** Do we get upset when a friend offers constructive criticism? Is our best friend careful around us because she doesn't want to hurt our feelings? Being thin-skinned is a huge distraction to building and expanding a relationship. In a solid friendship, there's an unspoken agreement that we let each other contribute to us. It's the "you have spinach in your teeth" kind of truth that separates friends from acquaintances. Let's not make friends wrong for something they're trying to do to help us. Sometimes responding with a

simple "Let me think about that" will give us the space to see and appreciate the intended contribution.

3. **Having to Be Right No Matter What.** Friendship isn't about who's right and who's wrong. It's not about getting what we want when we want it either. It's about give and take, and allowing for differences of opinions or styles. Being committed to a life of friendship means we respect our friends enough to hear their points of view and vice versa. Sharing and learning deepen friendships. We usually think our point of view is the right one. But if we've been dominating our friend with it, try a little *mea culpa*. Sometimes saying, "I'm sorry" is the best approach. See things from *her* perspective and feel *her* emotions. Isn't getting out of "ourselves" and into what's really important—the friendship—a better choice?

4. **Making It All About Us.** Friendship is a two-way street. Sometimes it may be all about us and other times all about her. But one thing's for sure; if we let our passions, interests, or upsets dominate our time together, we'll be on our way to one less friend. Camry, 47, a single mom, could only talk about her difficult teenage son when together with friends. Although her friends could commiserate and really cared about her trials, it was hard to have that be the only topic of conversation. Once she realized that she wasn't being included much anymore, Camry got the picture and broadened her topics of conversation.

5. **Comparing Ourselves to Others.** Comparing ourselves to our friends is treacherous. If we measure ourselves by our friend's success, it distracts us with sad-sack self talk. Wallowing in comparison keeps us from doing what we need to do to be our best and can lead to jealousy. If we're truthful and mus-

ter the courage to say, "I'm happy for you, I'm just envious," we'll stop focusing on our friend and start acting on what we can do to move ahead.

6. **Keeping Score.** Good friendships have a healthy give-and-take rhythm. Thinking everything has to be even sets up a tit-for-tat mentality. Aren't both parties responsible for balance in the relationship? For setting boundaries? Knowing when to say no? Allowing others to contribute to us? If we're mentally keeping score, try talking about it. We might say, "I'm feeling like I'm doing too much. Could you take care of that this time?" Anything can be resolved inside of open, honest communication. Give it a try!

7. **Being Too Busy.** The "I'm just too busy" excuse is one of the most insidious ways we rob ourselves of the opportunity to create and nurture friendships. Balance is an essential ingredient for happiness, and part of the balance we crave is provided by and with friends. Ask, "What am I so busy with?" If later in life we find ourselves lonely, wouldn't we have wished we had devoted a little more time to our friendships? Many say they can start again with a friend exactly where they left off, even after years or months go by. But wouldn't those relationships be even more satisfying with additional time dedicated to them? Taking part in our friends' lives requires mindfulness, planning, and sometimes even sacrifice. We have a choice.

Show Respect with Friendship Etiquette

When we're aware of our behavior and purposeful in our actions, we can face pitfalls and breakdowns head on in a way that honors the friendship. We call this Friendship Etiquette (FE). Like our personal *chi* or inner power, our FE powers our relationships with high-functioning workability. As children, we're taught simple rules of etiquette: to say "please" and "thank you" and to open the door for others. Likewise, FE shows we care for, and respect, not only each other but the relationship. Being polite and acting by the Golden Rule goes a long way in how others perceive and respond to us.

Overlooking FE practices in the heat of the moment is easy to do. But that can inflame and escalate an upset. Etiquette is basic. Without it we seem rude, unthinking, and intentionally hurtful. FE can soothe hurts and expedite healing.

Common reasons for failing friendships include when one friend becomes a broken record of complaints or dominates the relationship with her passions, interests, or upsets. Connect at the heart as well as the head. Even when we're conscious of our behavior and thoughtful about others' feelings, we each still bring our unique personality to bear. In some friendships, using humor is the emotionally intelligent thing to do. For others, handling things in knowing silence and allowing the other person to express her feelings is best.

Take Phyllis, 55, who went out to lunch with a colleague she hoped to become friends with. During the meal, Lisa, 53, shared that she was feeling badly about how a coworker treated her. Choking back her emotion, her eyes filled with tears. Wanting to make Lisa feel safe, Phyllis leaned over and whispered, "It's OK; I really do understand." Lisa sighed and let her feelings surface. "With that simple comment, the relationship began to deepen," said Phyllis. "I am so glad I gave Lisa permission to be human."

Knowing what to say or do when someone expresses emotion takes Friendship Etiquette. It requires being completely present and paying attention to her signals and our feelings. What does our intuition tell us? Often it's as simple as asking, "How would I want to be treated if

I were that person? What would make me feel accepted? Understood? Supported?" Putting ourselves in the other person's shoes helps us make the right choice.

There are also times when we instinctively know what we should do, but fear stops us. The fear of being too close, looking stupid, or not being accepted thwarts our intention to be a caring, supportive friend. We're likely to overanalyze our natural reaction. That's when we don't reach out, and the moment passes. The opportunity to show our compassionate side slips by. We usually kick ourselves later for letting our friend and ourselves down.

Diane's friend Sidonie is really good at understanding others' feelings. Due to busy summer vacations, they hadn't seen each other much, so Diane waited to talk to her after church one Sunday. Deep in conversation with another friend, Sidonie couldn't break away. After a few minutes, Diane left, thinking they'd catch up another day. Thirty minutes later Sidonie called and let Diane know how much she wanted to reconnect. It would have been so easy just to wait for the next Sunday, but Sidonie valued the friendship too much to leave things to chance. Her actions reinforced to Diane what a caring friend Sidonie is!

G✺TCHA! MOMENT

How to Move Through Difficult Times

Relationships provide tremendous joy and also some of the biggest challenges. If you find yourself in a tense moment with your friend, ask, "What outcome am I committed to?" "Am I committed to this relationship for the long haul?" "What is my stand in the matter?" "Is the friendship more important than my current point of view?" "Can I agree to disagree and move on?"

Getting clear about what really matters to you opens up new choices. Instead of giving up, arguing back, storming off, or shutting down, you might say, "I really value our friendship and hate to see us arguing...hate to see you suffering...hate to feel like this. I want to support you and work this out. Our friendship is important to me."

Are You the Friend You Want to Have?

Evaluating our part in a pitfall is critical. We must ask ourselves, "Do I add to or subtract from my friends' lives? Would I want me in my life? Am I faithful and loyal? Does my influence spur them on to be more than they thought they could be? Do I cheer their successes or support them in down times? Am I complaining, manipulative, or controlling?"

Most of us want friends who contribute to our lives—in both good and bad times. Life challenges friendships. Dynamics can change. When one of us suffers a setback, the relationship shifts. Adversities test us. We grow close or apart, depending on the understanding and support we're willing to give and receive. When we stick with each other, we lift up ourselves *and* our friends in the process.

A lot of people are unaware of how they "show up" in their friends' lives. If we want to keep friends, we've got to add value. Consider, "Am I giving and caring? Do I exhaust my friends with negative thoughts and constant excuses?" Our friends may be too kind or too tired to tell us to stop. Take the time to analyze things; be ready to make changes. When we're aware of what we want to bring to a friendship, we can be diligent about doing it. It doesn't mean we have to wait until we *feel* like doing something; we can simply do it because it's the right thing to do.

Vulnerability: A Friendship Imperative

Letting someone into our lives requires vulnerability. The veneer we have with acquaintances and colleagues easily rubs off when we become transparent and real with a friend. Being vulnerable is very scary. The more we reveal to someone, the more she knows our weaknesses, concerns, and sensitivities. This exchange can bond and seal a friendship for life, but it can also be fodder for hurting each other if we're not careful. It's risky! Holding the information as private and not using it against each other, in any way or at any time, is so important.

As we build new friendships, it's a good idea to test the water. A safe tactic is to share one or two intimate things at a time, rather than letting it all gush out at once. Start with something small to see how a new friend responds. Some people aren't able to keep confidences as well as they would like. The information may just be too much for them to keep private.

One woman shared with us that she told a friend her husband had been unfaithful. Upset and resentful, she used harsh and condemning words as she vented about him. The friend just listened and avoided the temptation to join in. She wisely recognized the need for confidentiality and avoided the temptation to share the information with mutual friends. Eventually the woman patched things up with her husband, and because her friend had acted with such sensitivity and prudence, their friendship actually strengthened.

That's a good reminder. If a friend is complaining, we can commiserate and say we understand. We might even share a similar frustration or offer pointers for calming down and getting through. But don't climb on the bandwagon with her! What a pitfall! FE 101 reminds us that *she* can call her husband lazy or inconsiderate, *she* can say that her child is ungrateful, and *she* can rant that her mother doesn't listen. But *we* can't degrade *her* people. She'll probably get past the upset with her spouse, be crazy with pride about her child's successes, and once again acknowledge her mother's love. We fulfill our role as a friend by fully supporting and not judging her or her family.

If we feel a friend is revealing too much information for comfort, we can ask her to stop. Knowing personal details is a huge responsibility, laden with pitfalls. Likewise, if *we're* thinking about sharing something very intimate with a friend, we must realize that not everyone has the same tolerances, values, and backgrounds. She may not be able to handle the information emotionally, spiritually, morally, or legally.

When we take someone into our confidence, watch how she responds and use it as a cue. While writing this book, Margaret shared with Diane an upset she was having in a major relationship. The details of the upset were very personal, but Margaret shared them carefully. Diane responded thoughtfully and tenderly. In the moment Margaret was willing to be vulnerable. But a few moments later, she became scared and concerned about being so forthright. She wished she hadn't said anything. What if she mended things with the person she was upset with, but Diane harbored resentment against that person for hurting her friend? What if Diane thought less of Margaret for being upset? Seeing the questioning emotion in Margaret's eyes, Diane hugged her friend. With that gesture, she brought compassion and love to the moment. A new, stronger bond resulted. Hurrah!!

G✸TCHA! MOMENT

Don't Throw the Baby Out with the Bath Water

Friend*shit* happens, but before you throw the baby out with the bath water, take time to reflect. Think back to the many experiences the two of you have shared. Remember the laughter, the tears, and the joy. Recall the places you've visited, the secrets and the feelings you've shared.

With that emotion and memory fresh in your mind, write down what your friend has meant to you. Recall all she has brought into your life. Weigh it. Contemplate it. Evaluate it. Chances are the positive far outweighs the negative, and you are better off with her *in* your life. Only you can decide.

Try to Make It Work, But Don't Be Afraid to Let Go

Most times, difficult issues between women can be resolved if both value the relationship and are willing to work through the pitfalls. If something has gone wrong, we can rely on our FE. Be the friend who finds common ground, seeks solutions, reaches out, or asks for forgiveness. True friendship does not let pride stand in the way of reconciliation. When the joys of the friendship are worth more than the recent pain, it's time to forgive and begin again.

When FE just isn't enough, we may need to take a time out, reflect, cool off, and let go of any IOUs in the friendship. Relationships take time, perseverance, and patience. They should add joy and dimension to life—not worry, agony, and strife. Ultimately, it's about finding a healthy balance of shared contribution and commitment.

"One of my friends got married to a man who is controlling and manipulative," says Amanda, 26. "I tried to talk to her, but it was impossible to get through. The wedding was a disaster. I was her maid of honor, so I threw her shower and bachelorette party, but it was all superficial, and I could feel the closure of our relationship. I hate that part because it doesn't feel good. She says she is happy, but I see how he sucks the life out of her, and she has nothing left to give. Unfortunately I've had to migrate away from her and make new friends."

Ending a friendship is difficult. Amanda seems to have done so in a way that let the relationship fade into the background, as hard as that can be. How do we end a relationship that has gone awry in an honorable way? When we think back to the friendships we've lost, we can ask ourselves, "Could I have done things differently? Are there amends I might have made? Are there upsets I should have forgotten?" We're not saying that we must overcome all breakdowns; there may be times when a friendship needs to end. At those times, however, it's so much healthier to end the friendship in a calm and thoughtful way rather than reacting out of anger, guilt, hostility, or shame.

Sometimes it can be helpful to disconnect from a faltering relationship and see if it can heal. We may need a few days, weeks, or even months to cool off. During the hiatus we can analyze what went wrong and acknowledge our role in the breakdown. Once we've taken the time to reflect, we can reach out and ask our friend to talk. Listening is one of the most precious gifts we give to another human being. We can ask clarifying questions to understand her point of view. The calmer we are, the better the two of us will feel.

Lolma remembers writing a letter to her friend Mariah, expressing a concern over something Mariah had said about her. In response Mariah told Lolma she had to end the relationship for awhile. A decade passed before they came back together.

"I don't remember who got in touch with whom, but we finally reconnected. We knew we couldn't be done because we were friends," says Lolma. "When we did get together, we decided not to dwell on what happened because we don't believe any good comes from processing things to death. We had to let go and get over it. Instead we decided to work on the lost time by filling each other in on what we missed in our lives. Now our relationship is better than ever!"

It's satisfying to know that friendships can heal, even years later. Only we can evaluate if a friendship is worth keeping, letting go of, or restoring. As Joseph Epstein writes in *Friendship: An Expose*, "Friends can be an immense complication, a huge burden, a royal pain in the arse…but without friendship, make no mistake about it, we are all lost."

Chapter 8

Creating a GOTCHA! Group:
Our Lifeline of Love, Fun, and Acceptance

The wisdom we've gained in being intentional about creating and sustaining *one-on-one* relationships also extends to a group of friends. The energy created when women gather to share passions and interests, or just for fun and relaxation, invigorates us. Groups create space for focused time and attention. Whether it's three women going out to lunch regularly, a dozen women engaged in a book club, or a service club volunteering for a cause, group gatherings nurture us and enhance our lives in so many ways.

Women overcome personal and professional obstacles to get together because we know we'll be better off once we do. And guess what? Our family and loved ones benefit as well. There's nothing like releasing the steam valve and gaining support, wisdom, and insight from a team of friends to support harmony on the home front!

Groups are stimulating, rewarding, and absolutely worth it. There's strength in numbers. Together women reveal thoughts and feelings and share a side of ourselves we may not otherwise. Inside a trusting, nurturing environment, where others are open and candid, we may find ourselves following suit.

Thirty-five-year-old Elizabeth enjoys gathering with a group of her friends for what they call "Friday Morning Bitch Breakfast." The women meet at a local restaurant and use this time to unwind from their week.

"It gives us a chance to 'bitch' about our problems and give advice," says the health and nutrition expert. "Even though it's not always the same group of women, we all agree that whatever is said at these cathartic breakfast sessions remains in confidence. We grant each other the freedom to 'let it all hang out' and even use each other for a 'sounding board' experience. We look forward to our special end-of-the-week time, which helps us hold it together during the week."

Each group of women has its own personality. Being around quick-witted women who thrive on humor, for example, can find us funnier than we even knew we could be. Margaret enjoys bringing humor to her women's networking group. Not only does making her colleagues laugh bring great satisfaction, it also begets a kind of group fun and frivolity. Women who are naturally prone to be funny follow her lead, while those less adept get to enjoy and participate in the experience.

With a unique combination of backgrounds and a richness of personalities, groups provide a clearing for personal growth and discovery. Groups of friends can bring us surprise, joy, growth, and the satisfaction of belonging. The diversity within a group opens us to new and different conversations, leading to fresh thinking and new ways of being.

Inside of a group, topics evolve that are not as predictable as in other more familiar interpersonal relationships. When with candid, compassionate women, we may be open to discussing troubles or concerns we'd normally avoid. Groups expose us to a variety of interpersonal styles that teach us about ourselves and others. We see how other women handle uncertainty, disappointment, happiness, and success. This wide-angle view offers us personal options in dealing with our own lives. By seeing through different eyes and experiences, we better understand our own worlds. As we take part and observe, we can adopt some of the traits, outlooks, approaches, or coping mechanisms we admire in others, while avoiding certain paths or less-becoming characteristics.

Being with other women has a way of making us braver and open to taking healthy risks. When others are willing to take a leap, we might too. The energy of a group could be what's needed to hop on the rollercoaster, take the dance class, select a unique necklace, or purchase an avant-garde piece of art. Groups can move us into new experiences and help us knock down barriers faster than we might on our own. They allow us to feel like our presence, perspectives, and participation matter. There's just something special about belonging!

Once a month Patty, 48, meets with a group of women whose children have attended the same school for nine years. Getting together for lunch or happy hour, they share their struggles with parenting, aging, dealing with family members, and bizarre ex-wives. Initially their kids and the similarities they shared drew them together—a friendship of convenience. Today the group still continues to bond. It's the appreciation for their differences that continues to draw them closer. They not only have different roots—hailing from India, Mexico, New Jersey, Nebraska, and California—they also have chosen different life paths. Some work; others don't. Some cook; others don't. Some drink in excess; some exercise in excess.

"We don't judge, we just love and appreciate each other's strengths," Patty says. "And we support or make light of our shortcomings. We laugh at the ironic, the absurd, and the sad events of our lives. It's the safety and the comfort of laughter that draw us closer. We 'get' each other, and there's nothing better than that kind of connection with one another."

What It Takes to Create a GOTCHA! Group

We have a responsibility when we're part of a group. Showing up, participating, being responsive, and communicating may sound simple, but they're essential for a group to survive and thrive. Members need to engage. While our participation may ebb and flow with other life priorities, we have a part to play in making the group work and be its best. As with individual friendships, it takes intention. What we receive typically far outweighs what we're asked to give.

Yet for some, a group setting may seem overwhelming, even threatening, especially at first. Groups provide a lot of stimuli and a variety of opinions. We can always test the waters and see what we're willing to tolerate.

Whatever groups we choose to be part of, we can greatly enrich the dynamic when we purposefully and openly talk about our commitment to be there for each other, today *and* tomorrow. Declarations are powerful. It's this stated intention that strengthens our commitment to each other and allows us to see our friends with the future in mind. It takes a paradigm shift and "being present" to view our female friends in this way. It's the same kind of thinking we engage in when we save up to buy a house or make a significant investment. Once committed to a future, we find ourselves thinking and acting with *that* future in mind. To have "women we want to grow old with," we need to act consistent with that vision today.

So what does it take to form a group of women who will Grow Old Together with Courage, Health, and Attitude—what we call a GOTCHA! Group? How do we find and sustain friendships in a group of women we care about? What do women do to support each other? How do three or more not become a crowd?

If we have a few girlfriends who already get together—be it for lunch, a walk, tennis, bunco, or a kids' play date—and we appreciate what they bring to our lives, we can cement the deal and ask them if they want to form a GOTCHA! Group. The difference between a group of friends who get together for an activity or each other's company and a GOTCHA! Group is the stated intention to Grow Old Together with Courage, Health, and Attitude.

We're *not* suggesting renaming existing groups, joining forces with other groups, or doing any activities differently. We *are* suggesting that we engage in a conversation about what's possible in being there for one another as we grow older—regardless of our current ages! How do we want to show up for and support each other as the months and years go by? Our commitment to each other creates the road map for growing old together with courage, health, and attitude. *GOTCHA!*

Finding Our Group Fit

If we're not yet part of a formal or informal network of women who gather in the name of friendship, exploring this prospect can prove fun. We can proactively search for existing circles of women who already meet, or form a group by inviting a few friends to dinner and suggesting getting together regularly.

Friendship groups let us explore common interests, share passions and perspectives, and reap the rewards of companionship, understanding, and love. While we may navigate an occasional upset, misunderstanding, or jealousy, these headaches are miniscule compared to the many benefits.

G✸TCHA! MOMENT

What's Stopping Us from Joining?

If being part of a group seems more exasperating than exhilarating, take heart. It may be that groups just aren't for you, but, before you ditch the idea, try to understand what's stopping you from engaging.

- ✸ Is it the time commitment? ("I've got too much on my plate to spend time with a group of women.")
- ✸ Did you have a prior negative group experience? ("I didn't belong to a sorority and have never been part of the 'in' group.")

※ Do you think you're bad at "small talk"? ("What a waste of time learning about shoes!")

※ Are you afraid of getting entangled in gossip? ("Will I be next?")

※ Do you believe you have nothing in common with the other women? ("I don't fit in.")

Such fears may mean you haven't found your "group fit." Being with like-minded women and sharing a similar passion or purpose can evaporate those concerns. When it's right, it's right!

Whatever the structure or format of our chosen group, what matters most is finding a place to belong and a space in which we feel supported, engaged, and valued. Our "group fit" will bring us new life that can last a lifetime! Here are ideas to help find your "group fit."

Round-Robin Events and Letters

How does a group of friends stay connected when they can't regularly get together in person? Over twenty years ago, three friends—Pamela, 62, from San Diego, and Faye, 64, and Mary, 62, both from Portland—began circulating a round-robin letter, a simple but meaningful effort! Each time they received the letter (yes, through the US Postal Service, not e-mail), they added their thoughts and experiences. Through their correspondence, they planned fun activities that allowed them to occasionally meet and spend time together.

Pamela shares, "Mary and I met at Lewis and Clark College in Oregon at age eighteen. Eight years later I met Faye. After I moved to San Diego, I wanted the two of them to get to know each other. It took some scheduling, but I was determined that they not only meet but love one another.

"We have been The Three Stooges ever since," continues Pamela. "Mary and Faye are very different personalities, and I'm the glue that has, over the years, smoothed the waters. We grew on one another and learned to accept each other's foibles. Our common values and commitment to our long-term relationship has allowed us to weather our distance and differences.

"We're regularly there for each other," says Pamela. "Faye was diagnosed with breast cancer, and, three months later, when she was deep into her chemo treatments, I also was diagnosed with breast cancer, so our chemo days overlapped. One weekend during our 'wig days,' she and her daughter came to visit. I picked them up at the airport in my purple convertible. We weren't very far from the airport when we both spontaneously pulled off our wigs. There we were: two bald 'eaglets' having a good laugh at ourselves.

"The three of us have girls' retreats in various locations, most of them filled with giggles. In our first San Francisco adventure, we returned again and again for the polenta and soup at one particular restaurant. Later we went to see 'Beach Blanket Bingo Goes to Babylon' and laughed so hard that I peed my pants, and we had to return to the hotel so I could change clothes!

"It's my intention to spend more precious time with my two precious friends who know me and love me no matter what! I am gladly, after all, the glue," says Pamela.

While these three friends initially got to know each other better through hard copy round-robin letters, their tradition could easily translate into a round-robin e-mail, Facebook, a private blog, or other form of communication. How fun it would be to pose a question and get your friends' reactions, or plant an idea and see what they say. There are so many variations on this theme, but it's the ongoing connection and spoken commitment to each other that make the difference between casual relationships and this kind of GOTCHA! Group.

Not Your Mother's Book Club

Ten years ago Kim, 48, who lives in the East Bay area of San Francisco, realized that her marketing job allowed her to meet women throughout the United States, but she only had a few friends within a ten-mile radius of her home. So Kim put together an e-mail list of women who lived nearby and suggested they form a "book club without a book." Kim envisioned a format for pure fun and joy. There would be no book to read, no dues to pay, and no commitment to even show up. But there would be plenty of opportunity for fun and communing when you did. Kim asked the group to invite other local women to participate. It didn't take long for the e-mail list to explode.

Today about 275 women take part in East Bay United Gals, affectionately called EBUG. They gather monthly for fun, camaraderie, and adventure. They've enjoyed a wide range of activities from Hula-Hooping lessons and wine tasting to palm reading and cooking with a chef. They even got together for a friendship salon to contribute ideas for this book!

"The women who attend EBUG are all interesting and enjoyable," says Kim. "There's no commitment, which takes the pressure off. I survey the group for ideas for the upcoming year and the women vote—the top dozen or so win. Those who suggest ideas normally take the lead in planning and hosting the event. Our gatherings attract thirty to sixty women who, over time, get to know each other and look forward to seeing each other. It's nice to have a safe place to talk about interesting subjects—and yes, we do talk about sex!"

Wondering what would happen when the kids went off to college and her corporate job ended, Sally, 58, the principal of a consulting company, knew she needed life outside of work. When a friend, who had lived overseas, complained that even with hints no one invited her to join their book club, they decided to start their own. Theirs would have different rules: wine at every meeting, no charge to attend, and members don't even have to read the book—plus field trips!

"When we read an English novel, the characters are always drinking tea, so we went to a botanical garden and the Twining Tea lecture about the history of tea," says Sally. "After reading *Loving Frank*, about a love affair of Frank Lloyd Wright's, we visited Falling Water, the most famous house he built in the middle of Pennsylvania.

"Now eight years later, there is very little turnover and a few more rules. The majority of us do read the book, but you can't complain if you haven't finished it because we talk about the ending. And we are tolerant. One woman hardly came for awhile due to her work and family commitments, but now that her daughter is off to college, she is faithful. When we read the book *The Woman Behind the New Deal: The Life of Francis Perkins,* we spent the whole night talking about women's issues and how far we've come. Our book club is a great way to get to know some really wonderful women. The first half hour is devoted to socializing. It's a support system for everything from getting shingles to surviving a death in the family or celebrating a big career accomplishment."

Another group of busy working women in Connecticut uses the book club format for discussing magazine articles.

"This started when my friend Ruth learned that Jessica, a colleague at work, was moving from New York City to Connecticut, and she wanted to help Jessica meet other women in Connecticut. So she got four of her close friends who live nearby to agree to take turns to meet at each other's home. As busy working women, we decided that we didn't have time to read books, but we *could* read a *Vanity Fair* article and discuss it," says Lynn, 52, who has worked for the same ad agency for twenty-five years. "These are really interesting women who are fun to be with. We're proof that women in their fifties can start something interesting. Jessica now has more friends, and we all share this fun commitment to each other."

Love cooking? How about a cookbook club? In this group each woman cooks a dish from the same cookbook and shares it with the group. While consuming their masterpieces, they review the directions and evaluate the recipes. They post pictures of the culinary delights on their blog.

Whether traditional or avant-garde, these kinds of clubs bring fun and conversation that extend beyond the meeting time. Vicki, 62, was caring for her ill mother when women from her book club brought dinner over to her family.

"It wasn't something I expected or asked anyone to do, but it proved to me how valuable these kinds of clubs can be," she says.

Mommy Groups

Young mothers who join mommy groups say that sharing thoughts, concerns, and feelings about motherhood and marriage provides perspective and insight. They feel connected having a variety of women to reach out to. The same can prove true with mothers of teens, young people serving in the military, or parents needing support of any kind.

Veronica, 40, is in two mommy groups, and is married with six children, ranging from age two to eighteen. Though incredibly busy, she finds time to devote to running one group and regularly taking part in the other.

"When I was younger, my sister was my best friend. Sadly she passed away when I was in my twenties, just as I met my husband, Tim," says Veronica. "He then became my best friend, and for a few years, I didn't think I needed more than my husband, my mother, and my daughter. I always admired women who had that lone lifelong friend since childhood. I don't have a friend like that in the same city I live in. Then when I joined a mommy group and later launched another, it became really clear that maybe God didn't mean for me to have that one friend who could be everything for me. Perhaps I needed something different. I believe that's why I was given twenty to thirty women who would all fill me up in different ways. Each of them brings me a different gift, and I hope I do the same for them. When I need to reach out to someone for help or support, I know one of them will pick up the phone or answer my text message."

Veronica's mommy group started with women from her church and today includes women from all backgrounds and cultures. She oversees the group through a password-protected online group, which she moderates. She posts gatherings and discussion topics. Each woman gets an e-mail to prompt her to go onto the site and share her thoughts and feelings.

"Because we all know it's for our eyes only, we really open up—sometimes saying things we would not even share with our husbands," says Veronica. "It's amazing how women really pour out their hearts when they have complete trust."

Due to the high level of intimacy, Veronica makes a point of reminding the group once a quarter about the importance of confidentiality and preserving the sanctity of the group. If someone is on the distribution list but not participating, either online or at in-person gatherings, it makes the other women uncomfortable.

"I occasionally have to ask a member to step out of the group for a while if she doesn't have time to participate," shares Veronica. "I work to stay connected with these women in other ways because I don't want our mommy group to appear 'cultish.' But as with any relationship, we are accountable for participating, and if we don't, it will die."

Along with the online community, the mommies meet regularly with their children for play dates in the park. While the kids play, the moms sit on the benches and discuss life. For example, Veronica, who has a teenage son and daughter plus three younger boys and a baby girl, didn't remember how difficult it was to mother a little girl. Being able to discuss raising Isabella with mothers of young daughters has been a tremendous support.

Veronica's husband, an attorney, damaged his spinal cord in an automobile accident a number of years ago. Though he can walk, he suffers from severe chronic pain. Another mom in the group has a husband who suffered a similar injury. Their ability to relate is a tremendous source of strength.

"The other mothers challenge me to be a better me," says Veronica, "We have a certain accountability to each other—to show up, to participate, to learn and grow, and to just be there to support one another. Yet if someone is going far afield, one of us speaks up and says, 'You know better' and then encourages a different attitude or behavior. Sometimes that's just what you need to get through something in a better way."

Once a month the group treats itself to "mommies' night out" at one of their homes. Everybody brings food, and they sit around in their socks for two hours eating and talking. Occasionally, they mix it up with game night. Veronica confesses, "We're a competitive group, so playing Pictionary, Catch Phrase, or Balderdash creates a fun and loud evening. My husband loves for me to go out with the girls because I come back a much healthier person!"

Bunco or Bridge, Anyone?

Leslie, 58, formed a monthly bunco group to forge better relationships at the school where she teaches second grade. There was a real division between the certified teachers and the support team. Today teachers, librarians, and speech therapists take turns opening their homes monthly to the group of twelve. The host makes or buys the meal. She also either purchases fun gifts with the six-dollar-per-player donation or forms a kitty for the winners of each hand.

"Sometimes we're silly; other days we're more sedate," Leslie says. "No matter the mood, it's a therapy session for all of us. We talk about personalities at work, though not in a mean-spirited way. And that's a big deal to me. I want upbeat women in our group who will look at the bright side and find a way to get through things."

Leslie says the bunco group has helped relationships at school because the women now "see" each other outside of what they *do* or *do not* do at work.

"We're three-dimensional because we've been to each other's home, and we've lived through and supported each other's trials and victories. When the bunco meeting gets cancelled, it's a big letdown. It's our time out. It takes no brainpower, and everyone gets excited about the prizes even though they are little trinkets. Sometimes we only get through a couple of the six rounds because we are talking and laughing so much. That's a real difference from when we started and were completely done in an hour. Now, even though we are done by 9:15 p.m. or so, people hang around talking in the street by their cars until 10:00 p.m.!"

The ability to get together with other women in a place that lets you be who you are is a huge outlet for most. And forging a common experience brings us closer.

"Games are really good for creating a shared memory without having to make small talk. If you have a bad day and don't want to talk about it, you can lose yourself in playing the game," says Sally, 58. "I help run a bridge club that attracts women who range in age from forty to eighty, who want to learn the game their parents played or just keep playing bridge. We make it OK to ask someone at another table how to bid; it's a safe haven to not look stupid if you are not sure how to play a hand and don't make the bid.

"We set the schedule at the beginning of the year, and each member has to host once every two years," Sally explains. "The hostess puts out wine, soft drinks, bridge mix, and dessert. We have an e-mail contact list and send out monthly reminders. If you sign up to play and can't make it, you get your own substitute. It's first come, first served—the first twelve women to sign up get to play. Bridge gives us something to do that's intellectual and inexpensive. Playing a game provides an icebreaker that's not about you; it allows you to think about something other than yourself."

From Birthday Gatherings to Investment Clubs

Six women from a Northern California neighborhood have been friends since 1981. Now in their fifties and sixties, they raised young children and took aerobics classes together. Back then money was tight, so they celebrated each other's birthday by throwing potluck dinners three or four times a year.

In 1989 Maddi, part of the six, suffered an unspeakable horror. One of her twins, Ilene, was abducted while walking home from middle school. Shortly after the kidnapping, the search volunteers and police department arranged a candlelight vigil and prayer service. Bidi, who's dubbed the group's spiritual advisor, arranged and led an ecumenical prayer service for Ilene's family, friends, and community. The six friends united in solidarity to support Maddi in this ritual, which has continued annually for more than twenty years.

In 1991 this same group began learning about and investing in the stock market together. Their casual birthday gatherings developed into "Savvy Ladies Investing Money." Even with some women moving out of the neighborhood, divorcing, and starting or changing careers, they continue to meet to talk about their investments.

"We try to do everything ourselves, from researching stocks and determining our investing theory to setting the rules and deciding when to sell," says Pam, "We rotate officers and, within the last few years, hired an accountant. Our individual investments have grown from twenty-five dollars a month to ninety-five dollars a month. We've all received a huge education and a nice monetary reward."

To be successful Pam says the women have had to pay attention to group dynamics. "So we don't get frustrated or feel like we're competing for attention prior to the meeting, we give ourselves thirty minutes to visit before beginning. Of course we still celebrate our birthdays but now at restaurants. Our friendships continue to evolve, just as we do."

A number of years ago, Kathy, one of the members, let the group know that her husband had been diagnosed with late-stage colon cancer. While others wanted to talk about how they could help, Kathy didn't want that. Again the group had to learn to adjust and go on.

"Kathy would only say whether things were good or not," says Pam. "She never broke down. The rest of us felt a little hurt and very helpless. After a year and a half, her husband went into remission. Only then did Kathy let herself become emotional. We had an *aha!* moment. We realized that this was how Kathy had to deal with things; it wasn't personal. That was an interesting learning process for all of us."

Pam says the group recognizes that there will be subsets of friendships within the larger group. "Some of us get together outside of our birthday and investment gatherings to hike, shop, or just have coffee," she says. "Those who don't see other members except at the monthly meetings aren't jealous. They're just in a different spot.

"While I have lots of friends I meet for a glass of wine or a movie, there's something wonderful about having a handful of girlfriends who gather regularly and really know and understand each other. With our strong, enduring connection, we've continued to meet each other's changing needs over time. Most of us are now nearing sixty, our children are on their own, and some of our parents have died. Yet I know these women will be there for me no matter what. I will travel with them when I'm older and on my own. And if I'm in the hospital, they are the ones who will make sure my face is waxed and I look presentable! We would do anything for each other, and I feel so blessed by that."

Slumber or "Slumper" Party, Anyone?

Who remembers slumber parties as a child? They were lots of fun, and we begged our moms to let us have friends stay overnight. We talked about school, boys, and passions. Problems were solved, support gained, and we literally laughed till we cried.

Lynda, a woman in her fifties in Margaret's networking group, never had sleepovers as a child. Because she found it easier to befriend boys, she wasn't interested in female friendships. Now in her forties, Lynda is expanding her relationship with women and doing the fun things she missed as a child. She put together a women's sleepover weekend for the entire networking group.

"Communicating through our group website, everyone responded with much enthusiasm," said Lynda. "Some women are cooking breakfasts, and others are planning fun activities for the weekend. Even though all can't participate for the entire weekend, women are showing up when they can and participating at a level that works for them."

Margie, 70, agrees that the best way to create an instant rapport is to do an overnight stay and breakfast the next morning. "I have a group of women in the Boston area that I've been meeting with for fifteen years. We do something fun at night and then share breakfast the next morning. We've done this in Cape Cod in Massachusetts and at the Norman Rockwell Museum in the Berkshires. These rituals are still some of my most cherished times.

"It takes clear intentions and then rituals to keep the flame burning in our friendships," Margie says. "Relationships are the secret sauce of life."

For a fun slumber party game, try the Ungame. This is a set of cards that engages us in questions about everything from our proudest moments to our deepest fears. Or we might ask friends to take turns listing three of their most important accomplishments, something that took courage, stamina, or stick-to-itiveness. One caveat: We *can't* say anything a child or spouse did; this has to be something *we* achieved and *we're* proud of! When Margaret played she shared the day she found herself at the deep end of the swimming pool and overcame her fear of being underwater. With this gutsy triumph, she became her daughter's backyard swim instructor!

Not up for a slumber party? Maybe a "slumper" party will counteract those "down in the dumps" feelings. Having a few girlfriends over to keep us company, talk through our troubles, and hear their troubles may be just what we need to emerge from our slump with a whole new 'tude!

Spiritual Study Clubs

It may be the original book club—women getting together in small groups for fellowship and to gain a deeper understanding of God's word. Women who share a common belief have an instant bond. Praying together and for one another is such an intimate way to grow friendships and create a sense of belonging.

G✸TCHA! MOMENT

Group Roles and Responsibilities

Successful groups require ground rules. Openly discussing expectations helps to avoid confusion or upsets. Ask yourself:

❀ What's your group's purpose?

❀ Will you meet regularly and where?

❀ Are there formal accountabilities for attendance, start times, rules of order?

❀ Is there a formal membership process?

❀ Are there dues?

❀ How will leadership responsibilities be handled?

Volunteering for a Cause

Giving back to the community is important. Whether we're joining a nonprofit organization board or volunteering in our neighborhood, doing something out of the goodness of our hearts is not only rewarding but a great way to meet like-minded girlfriends.

Kathy, 61, a jewelry store owner with thirteen grandchildren, says, "Friendship is so much easier when our values align. I've met wonderful women I never would have known because of volunteer groups and boards I've joined. Because we share the same intentions and interests, we have an immediate bond. Even after I've resigned a position, I'm grateful my friendships have remained intact because these are women I really care about."

We never know when a volunteer project will result in a lifelong friendship.

One of Margaret's dearest relationships evolved out of inviting a Japanese college student to live in her home. Her neighbor Julia was also hosting a student, and the two women met synchronizing a carpool schedule. That chance meeting led to twenty-plus years of friendship. They've shared the experiences of holiday dinners, the growth of their children, marriages, and the birth of grandchildren. Today they enjoy philanthropic adventures and the intimacy years of friendship can bring.

Their love for each other is very special, and they vow to grow old together. Margaret also remained dear friends with the Japanese student, who's now married to an American man. They visit on the phone, and her two young daughters are a special bonus to Margaret.

To keep connected with women in her community, Margie, a single, retired railroad manager in her sixties, joined the Homemakers Council. This service group has nineteen chapters throughout Nassau County, Long Island, New York. She networks, enjoys monthly speakers, attends special events—and generously gives to others.

The Homemakers Council members have handed out new socks at a veterans' hospital, supported a home for unwed mothers, and made Care Bears for children who have suffered the loss of a loved one. These women do for others what they *can't* do for themselves—the true definition of helping!

Leesa, 53, uses volunteering to foster friendships. One of her special interests is helping out at food and wine festivals.

"I volunteer at four or five of these special events each year, and I've met wonderful friends," she says. "We're out in beautiful countryside, and within an hour, you feel like you're on a vacation. Then afterward we head to a great restaurant for dinner."

Seven years ago Margaret joined a San Diego women's philanthropy group. She was clear that the purpose of joining the group was as much about enjoying the friendship of new women with similar interests as it was engaging in significant philanthropy. Over the years she has taken on many leadership roles in the organization, from being on the board to serving on its committees. Her involvement in the organization has been very rewarding and resulted in relationships that extend beyond the committee work. It's exciting to share common interests while at the same time exploring and expanding relationships. Having like intentions creates a fabulous GOTCHA! Group possibility.

G✸TCHA! MOMENT

Entering a Group as a Newbie

Joining a new group of women can be intimidating. It's natural, at first, to feel like you don't fit in, but be patient and kind to yourself and others. It takes time to become part of something, and it's only by sharing the experience that you gain a sense of belonging. Here are a few steps you can take to ease your way into a group.

✸ When you feel like hiding in a corner, look for someone who seems welcoming and introduce yourself.

✸ Show respect for the women who have been in the group awhile and calibrate your expectations. Don't get discouraged if you don't feel like you instantly belong. Having an open attitude allows the circle to naturally widen and include you.

✸ Talk about *them*. Ask questions. Show your support and interest through your words, facial expressions, and body language.

✸ Be a player and follow protocol.

✸ Avoid the conversation killer, "My other group didn't do it like this." Be open to new ways and demonstrate your support.

✸ Don't leave early because you feel "out of it." Hang in there to listen and learn.

✸ Ask someone you meet if she'd like to visit over a cup of coffee.

Remember, each woman in the group had to start somewhere, just like you. When you see another newbie trying to fit in, befriend her, and bring her along!

Group Dynamics: How Not to Make Three or More a Crowd

Whether one-on-one or in a group, relationships sometimes present challenges. Knowing how to negotiate the relationship "with the group," as well as with individual members, calls for another level of awareness and energy. We're all responsible for the dynamics of the group. The sisterhood of support and bonding is well worth the effort.

Beware. Certain group dynamics can lead to cliques and pettiness. If we want a GOTCHA! Group to work, we must recognize when we're not playing nicely in the GOTCHA! sandbox. Things won't always go as we wish, so give each other some space. Don't harbor resentment. Discuss problems, what's causing them, and how the group can resolve them. One or two bad experiences aren't enough to spoil your GOT-CHA! Group. Needless to say, if we allow negativity to pervade, most women will not have the patience to endure. Taking responsibility for the group dynamic is a very high level of leadership. Sometimes there's only one person willing to do this. Ideally each woman is equally responsible for creating engagement and harmony that entices us to return and participate fully. When that occurs, enjoy the miracles!

Deborah, 48, has a group of eleven friends who all worked for a boutique search firm in Atlanta. At least twice a year, they schedule a get-together, such as a Sunday brunch or Friday happy hour.

"Someone steps up to make the arrangements," she says. "We spend three to four hours catching up. There have been personal challenges like when someone has gotten laid off or promoted and another didn't, but we figured out a way to discuss that and move on. We've got an informal ritual that we spend the first ten minutes bitching, griping, and complaining. So instead of having an elephant in the room that no one dares bring up, we put it out there. There are plenty of reasons why each of us could have let this time become divisive. But this practice of letting the negativity come forth allows us to rely on gallows humor. Once we've all purged, we go on to talk about other things. That's built a trust and a bond that has kept us coming back."

Sandye, 53, realizes that women can be competitive, so she doesn't force the group dynamic. "I see who needs to talk and then just kick back and let them say all they need to say," she says. "I don't try to compete in any way. I've learned it's not about me; it's about them. So I just let my friends talk, and I listen."

There are many ways to become and remain part of a group. While learning to get along with unique personalities can be challenging, it almost always pays off. Just knowing there are women who are in our corner and available brings comfort, security, and hope. Hard times become more bearable and good times even better. Consider it a sorority for life. Groups of any size let us talk about our intention to Grow Old Together with Courage, Health, and Attitude—GOTCHA! To be there for each other no matter what! Seal the deal and feel the commitment grow. Why would we want it any other way?

Chapter 9

Group Rituals and Retreats

Some women share a practice of meeting regularly for the sole purpose of forming deeper friendships and contributing to each other's life. They're practicing the art of being, not doing, and in the process they grow and add meaning to their lives and relationships.

"About seventeen years ago, I began meeting with a number of women who wanted to share a ritual of getting together with the same group of women once a month to update each other on their lives and form deeper relationships," says Andrea, 55, a government relations attorney.

"It was all started by a woman who was tired of having only shallow conversations with friends she'd run into at the grocery store or sporting events," says Andrea. "After talking it over, she decided to invite about a dozen women to meet every other week in a room at a local church. From the beginning we started every meeting with a ritual of giving everyone five to ten minutes to check in and share about what was going on in their lives. To help us stay organized, we used to pass around a candlestick to symbolize when someone had the floor. We're not trying to accomplish anything; our only agenda is no agenda. It's just a time to talk and connect.

"I am an external processor, so it's great to have someone, other than my husband, whom I can trust and who can be a mirror for me. We can share openly in our group because we have a very important understanding that anything that is said in the group doesn't leave the room. We have honored that trust code for all these years now, and it gives us a lot of freedom to share deeply personal thoughts and process important moments in our lives.

"While the group started with twelve women, it's been stabilized for years with five of us who meet about three or four times a year now, although we e-mail each other very frequently. It's hard if we miss a meeting and then need to get caught up. Sometimes one or more of us have to move mountains to make a meeting. We've had serious discussions about so much, from divorces to difficult children to deaths and births. We've held each other in tears of joy and in tears of sorrow. The existence of our group is such a living force now that we gain great strength from it and each other in times of difficulty, even when we aren't together."

Once the group realized they all had turned fifty over the past few years, they decided to take a trip to Santa Cruz, California, to visit one of their members who had moved. She has since returned to Maine, and the group was thrilled to greet her back home.

"We spent a week together with no schedule and one rule: not to rush," explains Andrea. "We took turns cooking, watched movies, walked along the beach, and picnicked in a coastal park. In the beginning we started the day with a check-in but decided we didn't want anything distracting us from being in the moment. This was a time to relax and rejuvenate. At dinner we all took turns saying how we felt. The first night I said 'tentative,' and by the last night, I said 'acceptance.' As wives, mothers, and employees, our identities can become wrapped up in taking care of everyone else, and it's easy to forget who we are on an individual basis. For this special week, we were not being parents, wives, or career women. We were simply women spending time with other women.

"I struggled with leaving my family at home," notes Andrea. "My older daughter and husband were both supportive, but my younger daughter didn't think Mom going away by herself was such a good idea. I tried to help her understand that it would be better for all of us if I did. I needed to replenish my well.

"What I have realized is that, while I love my children dearly, I don't think relying on children, even older children, for peer friendship is healthy. They cannot give me the affirmation of who I am that girlfriends can because they don't have that perspective. There are certain things about me they don't want to know and certain things I don't want to share. My husband is my rock, but he doesn't want to be the only one to take care of me. Every year he goes on an annual adventure with two college friends, so he understands my need for girlfriends."

Annual Adventures for Respite and Rejuvenation

What are girlfriends for if not to set aside "me time" with? There's something about encouragement from other women that gets us to say "yes" to ourselves. Finding a way to refresh and rejuvenate can be so difficult, but when girlfriends are on the case, a force larger than ourselves makes it doable. It's wonderful to plan, scheme about, and look forward to these special times.

Liz, 54, and three of her friends, who live scattered across the country, set aside seventy-two hours each summer for a sailing respite. They provision Susan's wooden sloop in Maine with great food and wine, linen napkins, and small gifts for each other. After sailing during the day, they drop anchor by evening near an island, walk along the beach, skinny dip, and work through "serious baggage."

"For more than twenty years, we've rearranged our lives to share this gift of time," says Liz. "It's not ever easy, but it's always worth it. We each balance the foursome in different ways. We are each so different but such dear friends. I usually arrive exhausted after working a sixty-five-plus-hour week. Susan, who owns the boat, is all about precision and perfection and a wonderful ally and supporter. Sid's an amazing sailor and very giving. She's nurturing, calm, cool, and collected—a healer. No one can put me back together like she can. And Cate has held positions as captain of offshore sail-training vessels and an Outward-Bound instructor. She's led all kinds of women's expeditions over the years. Her experience and knowledge are just amazing. I've been a lover of natural history and teach about the sky and the sea. Each of us brings special gifts and experience to our sailing adventure, and we treasure them all!"

When these four women set sail on the forty-three-foot long, seven-foot wide sailboat, their personalities combine, and a working team emerges. With each having her distinct role, they've learned what they need to do to find harmony.

"We can each be impossible at times," said Liz. "I learned that when I first arrive and am still wired from my city job, it's time for me to step back, go down below to take a nap, and give everyone some space. I can't perform at the level of precision that Susan needs in the moment, so I'm better off out of the way. When we're sailing downwind and things are easier, I go forward, sit on the bow, and just take it all in. It took me years to figure this out, but we each do what we need to do to make sure the friendship stays tight."

Patty, 48, and her five friends from across the country have gotten together annually for twenty-five years.

"We always do fun things, but whether at a spa, birthday party, or wedding, what we do best is talk," she says. "We reminisce, laugh, and vision for the future. When we think five minutes have passed, we look at our watches and realize it's been hours.

"While all very different, we share a bond that has us adore each other," Patty continues. "Even so, certain things annoy us, like when one person tries to impose her political views. But when we're up-front about what bothers us, the bonds grow even stronger. We're able to laugh at each other's quirkiness.

"My sons like to see me socialize. I think it's important that I serve as a role model by making friends a priority. That doesn't mean my friends come before my family. Sometimes I have to focus more on one aspect of my life than the other. When that's gone on too long, I make myself step back and rebalance."

G✺TCHA! MOMENT

A Starter Set of Ground Rules

GOTCHA! Groups work best if you and others can let go of preconceived notions about friendship, not jump to conclusions, or get stuck in your opinions. Group interaction demands a more sophisticated level of relationship and the ability to *put up* with more than we would normally tolerate. Try not to have preconceived ideas. Leave yourself open to what might be possible when you make a commitment to be part of a group. Consider these simple recommendations as operating instructions to protect you and your friends from "losing it" with each other when you're together:

✺ Be giving and generous (the more you are, the more others will be).

✺ Don't judge or gossip.

✺ Communicate honestly and kindly; offer feedback gently.

✺ Forgive easily and with a loving heart.

✺ Laugh, laugh, laugh at yourself and each other.

Forming a Getaway Group from Scratch

If we're longing get away from it all with a group of women but don't know where to turn, we can start with the friends we have and create a ritual. DeeDee, 42, did just that when she was about to turn thirty-nine. She had several college friends who she met annually for sporting outings, but she lacked local girlfriends to "escape" with.

"On a whim, I decided to start an annual hot springs weekend for girlfriends," she says. "I reached out to twenty women, between the ages of thirty and fifty. Many were moms of children who my kids play with. They all agreed they wanted to take part. Like me, many said they hadn't had that kind of girl connection since their college days. So I chose a hot springs resort that's like a sanctuary, with yoga, meditation, massage, and a clothing-optional policy that I thought most of the women would be OK with.

"We've now gone on a hot springs weekend for three years," continues DeeDee. "We leave early on a Friday and return by dinner Saturday so our husbands get a break on Sunday. We plan all the meals ahead of time to prepare in the beautiful kitchen. We hang out on a gorgeous veranda where we eat and talk. It's a beautiful blending of experiences that's been so rewarding. The group gets along great, and individual friendships have formed within the group. Women go off hiking together or decide to take time to chat privately in subgroups of two or three. It's so therapeutic to be with women friends, laughing and hearing what they're going through. I'm really hard on myself, so it's good to know that others feel guilty as moms addicted to smartphones, or wishing they had stronger libidos. For two days we don't have to be wives, moms, or business professionals. We indulge in pure selfishness. Thank goodness there's lots of laughing.

"My advice if you don't have a group like this is to form one. Don't be afraid to put yourself out there and ask women you know if they're interested in joining you to do something rewarding and fun. That's the beauty of e-mail—you can reach out with little effort and start something great!" says DeeDee.

Women's Circles

Another vehicle women use to gain strength is a women's circle, where they literally sit in a circle to share thoughts, feelings, and perspectives. This format provides a structure for listening, which leads to better conversations.

Donna, 53, has been part of what she calls "Circle" for six years.

"Twice a year we rent a beach house for three days," Donna explains. "We arrive on Friday evening, have dinner together, and then sit around and talk. On Saturday morning, we enter into a dialogue circle beginning with a ritual or meditation. Afterward we have a thirty-minute check-in on what's been going on in our lives."

To the women in the circle, the time is sacred. They pass around antlers—that Donna discovered one year when the circle was on a walk together—instead of a talking stick.

"We go into Circle being fully present, which gives us the gift of intimate connection. We always come away with a different perspective or a new idea. And there's an even power base. No one leads Circle or is in charge of how things go, but at any time one of us is thinking ahead and takes the lead. There's always someone to lead and someone to follow. It's usually a healing experience."

Ideas for the circle sometimes come from the check-in. Other times a member brings a discussion topic to the group. One year Donna proposed "joy" and how it did or did not manifest in each of their lives. They talked about what they did to cultivate joy and the full spectrum of emotions, from rage to happiness, that allow them to be whole.

After the morning circle, the women break for lunch, take a walk, and then resume their dialogue. At the end of the day, they again walk on the beach, cook, and watch movies. Once, when they wanted to be more creative, they made collages of who they wanted to become.

Each woman in the circle finds a niche she fills for the weekend. "One of us arranges for the beach house, another plans breakfast, someone else brings movies or another creative thing for us to do," explains Donna. "We're totally OK with our roles or with giving up our roles. There is no competition. We are all there to support one another.

"While a few of us may see each other outside of Circle to have dinner or catch up with one another, our core relationship is the relationship to the wholeness of Circle. That's where the power lies. We are not necessarily best friends, but we support and learn from one another.

"We've had varying levels of what members want to commit to in Circle—some want more intimacy; others want to meet more frequently. But one thing is for sure; we never disagree on our commitment to protect Circle," says Donna.

For Donna, the power of the circle lies in knowing she's not alone. "I had a serious medical emergency a few years ago," she says. "One of first things I did was to ask my partner to call the women in my circle. I wasn't asking for them to visit but to hold me in their thoughts and prayers. That's what we do for each other. No matter what else happens in life, no matter who dies or who leaves, we know Circle is going to be there because we have made a lasting impression in one another's life."

Chapter 10

*Friends at Work: The Two **Do** Mix*

Sometimes one of the easiest places to find friends is in a work-related setting. Many of us spend so much time tending to our jobs that it makes sense to take advantage of opportunities to meet people with similar interests and backgrounds.

"Knowing and counting on friends at work makes it a richer and more delightful place to be," says Elizabeth, 34. "Friends at work are a blessing, a neutral factor that allows you to be yourself. They're not like the political or management aspects in a workplace."

"The professional environment is a great way to find and cultivate friends with similar career paths and interests. It provides a support network of a different but valuable kind," says Francie, 65, a long-time entrepreneur.

While some suggest keeping our work and personal lives separate, according to a growing body of research, having friends at work is not only acceptable but even recommended. Long-recognized studies by the Gallup organization show that "having a best friend at work" is a real job satisfier. People who socialize with work colleagues in and outside of the workplace are more engaged than those who don't. In fact Gallup found that people with a "best friend at work" are seven times more likely to be engaged in their jobs and are more apt to have satisfied customers.

Making friends at work also reduces stress. University of Rochester Medical Center researchers found that people who don't feel socially supported at work are two to three times more likely to experience depression. Because they share the same kind of stress, co-workers can provide a protective layer of understanding and security. This results in higher productivity. And, having friends at work makes people want to stay in their jobs longer.

Though employers used to frown at the idea of fraternizing at work, new-generation employees want work "to be a place where their life is being lived out," according to a human resource management online diversity focus area report.

"When young professionals are starting out and working together, they often confront the same work and personal milestones, challenges, and discoveries. They build a bond that can last a lifetime," says Marjorie, a retired health care executive, who notes that some of her closest friends today, at age sixty, are from her early career days. "I had the pleasure of working on very exciting projects with some good friends. That shared experience and mutual respect creates a deeper friendship than a 'meet in the bar' kind of friendship."

Work-initiated relationships offer opportunities to connect in ways that other relationships can't. It's the focus, challenges, breakdowns, and leaning on each other to overcome professional obstacles that provide the backbone for deep, lasting relationships.

The benefits of having workplace friends—even if we can't disclose everything—far outweigh the potential risks. Let's face it, our business lives may be rewarding, but they're not always easy. The workplace is a perfect petri dish for fear, competition, and stress. The pressure of meeting deadlines; achieving quotas/financial results; and pleasing bosses, clients, and customers can be challenging and exhausting. Having one or more women who can be a sounding board, cheering squad, and support system can make our work lives more manageable and fun.

These women serve as our workplace intention holders. They're in our corners, watching out for us. Their "count-on-ability" gives us confidence, comfort, renewal, and perspective. Because we're in the trenches together, we've developed a "knowing" as work friends that can't be replicated with friends and family outside of work.

"Friends at work provide a shortcut to support and understanding around work issues," says Sylvia Lafair, Ph.D., author of *Don't Bring It to Work*. "You can talk to colleagues about work issues, and they know immediately what's going on. You don't have to invent a container for them. They know the culture and speak the same language. You can de-stress quickly and easily. But we have to realize it's not about getting people to agree with us but being heard without having to explain everything."

Arlene, a fifty-something regional vice president for a pharmaceutical company, gravitates toward those at work with whom she can be open and honest.

"It's a combination of perceptions that come from words, body language, and reactions that tells me whether someone is a good match," she says. "It's important to be genuine and transparent because people can tell when you're not. Occasionally I'll think, 'Oh my God, I said too much.' But then I tend to forget about it and go on. I've found that if you have friends at work, you don't need a psychiatrist. Having others to talk to helps you work things out and not feel like the only one experiencing something. They help you feel normal."

Elizabeth, 34, rarely talks to her husband Ryan about work. "My work friends understand the 'work thing' and are so valuable to me," she says. "They get the nuances and know the players, which my husband doesn't. I can go out to coffee or lunch with them and start in the middle of a sentence, and they get it!"

"Some of my closest friends have been work colleagues," says Shellie, 65. "They are my sisters, mentors, shrinks, and Dutch uncles. They'll tell me to get off my high horse and remind me that I don't always have to be right."

Avoid Career-Limiting Mistakes

With all the benefits they afford, workplace friendships do hold the risk of something going sour that could have negative ramifications. It's important to remind ourselves about the value of being prudent and keeping some separation between work and private lives. There are things that just can't be discussed and other things that are better left unsaid. Knowing when not to cross the line is critical.

"I can see the argument that you don't want to have a negative friendship experience interfere with a work relationship," says MargE, 26, who works in the family advocacy unit of a military hospital. "But if you just ease into a friendship, then you should be able to figure out each other's boundaries and not have a problem with it."

Author Sylvia Lafair, Ph.D., says that as with everything in life we have to be responsible about how we act and react at work. In her book, she reports how the patterns of behaviors that we've developed in our personal and family lives repeat at work, often to our detriment.

"The behaviors we developed for security and survival in early childhood will come out in the workplace when the anxiety and stress heat up," she says. "We naturally go to those old patterns of being the pleaser, victim, bully, martyr, or overachiever. These patterns *are* transformable *if* we are aware of them, just as we might be aware of our Myers-Briggs personality tendencies. We can use what we know to become the healthy opposite. For example, a pleaser might become a truth-teller, and an overachiever can become a creative collaborator."

What does this have to do with making friends at work? Every relationship, whether with an individual or a group, has particular circumstances that we must be aware of. A work community can be compared to a family. Certain things can only be said to certain people and then in the strictest of confidence. Be aware and be responsible in the work setting. We don't want someone we feel close to cajoled into agreeing with us as we might have done with our older sister. It pays not to get into circular negative talk about our boss or colleagues, as we might have done about a controlling parent. And if we're leaders, avoid showing favoritism that can stir jealousy. Find friends at work who are self-aware and mature. And avoid getting pulled into things that are career limiting by taking sides.

Sometimes workability in a job setting is as simple as putting yourself in the other person's shoes. "This isn't high school," Sylvia says. "So using superlatives, like saying someone's your 'best' friend, can elicit a reaction. Using 'good' friend promotes inclusion versus exclusion. Be sensitive; these are people we see every day of the work week."

Sylvia suggests expanding our circle of work friends to include people we might not ordinarily reach out to. Invite someone new to lunch or an after-hours outing. "You never know what piece of your puzzle she holds," she says. "The person who is your 'petty tyrant' and annoys you the most is a person that you can learn from—about your work and yourself.

"We may want to share everything, but telling the truth is not the same as spilling your guts," continues Sylvia. "Friendship at work is an art form that demands practice. It takes one or two times of tripping over ourselves or having a confidence violated to learn to modulate our behavior. If we feel the slightest tinge of nervousness and anxiety about something we are ready to say or do, we should hesitate on the side of caution."

Lois, 73, has worked with one of her employees in her therapy practice for the past seventeen years. The close friendship they've developed hasn't come easily.

"When she first came to work for me, she had a reputation for not getting along with other employees, but I wanted to help her grow and develop," says Lois. "We struggled, and sometimes still do, in places where our personalities don't mesh. We're committed to get through the 'stuff' that comes up. She's very loyal, and we've worked through some very tough crises over the years. In the process, our friendship has grown."

Personalities and politics can spoil our friendships at work. Avoid obvious pitfalls, like gossip. Always go to the source to find out what the person is really thinking and feeling. Pause before reacting in trying situations. How would we behave if one of our friends at work got promoted and we didn't? What if a friend becomes our manager or vice versa? How will we behave if we have a disagreement at work with a friend we are also close to outside the office?

"Having each other's back is crucial to a supportive network," says Lois. "Learning not to take things personally and realizing that we each have our own ways of doing things make for better friendships."

"It's key to respect each other at work," says Marjorie. "When we can do that, our friendship challenges in the workplace will be much more manageable."

MargE presents a novel idea. "If you don't like someone at work, try being her friend. Don't end something before it begins," she says.

If things still don't work out, be careful not to burn bridges. We've all experienced having to lie in the bed we've made, so to speak, and the effort it takes to "remake" that bed. How many positive experiences does it take to neutralize the impact of a negative one? Lots!

When we successfully navigate the friendship waters at work, we create a great place for support, celebration, and laughter. That makes for, what can feel like a daily grind, a more pleasant and enjoyable experience!

G✳TCHA! MOMENT

Setting Boundaries in the Workplace

Poet Robert Frost gives us permission to set boundaries and use "good fences" to establish lasting and working relationships. Don't be afraid to say what works and doesn't work for you. Here are some possible scenarios.

✳ Be a Vegas girl: Let your work friends know that what happens at work stays at work. In other words, let's not drag work issues into private circles where you may have mutual friends.

* Get clear for yourself the three things you'll never discuss in the office, for example, your exes in Texas, management issues, anything that starts with "It's not fair..."

* Never drink more than two glasses of wine—or do anything else that affects judgment—at work socials. Recognize the difference between gossip and sharing.

Building That Nine-to-Five Support System

So how do we build a nine-to-five support system? Start by getting to know the women we work with better. Invite a colleague, consultant, or someone we meet at a business function for coffee or lunch. There we'll have the opportunity to share values, interests, and passions.

"Getting out of the business setting provides another way to see someone's strengths and vulnerabilities," says Pat, 64. "For me, it's essential that I know I can trust someone before I become friends with her at work. I need to learn early on if the person is someone who will keep my confidences or turn around and misrepresent something I've said."

To Deborah, 48, finding friends at work comes from *being* a friend before expecting friendship in return. "You have to be willing to be open and real," she says. "Having a friend at work doesn't mean you can't bring your personal life to work. It's not about compartmentalizing. While you have to do that somewhat until you get to know someone, you can still be authentic. One of my dearest friends started as a work colleague. At first she intimidated me because she always had a stoic expression on her face. Then one day I said something with a British accent, and she responded back in kind. That playfulness broke the ice, and we became extremely close. Work friends help carry us through our professional *and* personal lives, so I don't believe we should draw such harsh lines between the two. We have to be aware of boundaries, but as you get to know and trust someone, you can slowly reveal more of who you are outside of work."

Demonstrating that we'll "be there" for a colleague to confide in is essential in fostering confidants. We can offer to have a chat on our way home from work or meet for coffee on a Saturday to talk through a thorny situation. Along with being a sounding board, we can provide that all-important "other" point of view, allowing our friend to see things through a different lens.

"Women I work with have brought me amazing value," says Deborah. "They're the ones who talk me down off the ledge, so to speak. We've all had those 'the world is out to get me' moments. A work friend helps us think things through, vent, gain perspective, provide context, and regulate our emotional reactions. She might say, 'I see why you might think this, but here are five reasons why this may not be a vendetta against you.' She helps get us to solid ground and find our footing to move forward yet another day."

As in any friendship, sometimes we're the sage; sometimes we're the student. That means we get to teach as well as learn, inspire, and perspire. We can be brilliant one moment and dull the next. If we have true friends, they'll see all sides and recognize when to let us fly and when to catch us so we'll have softer landings.

"I relish it when a woman at work comes to me for validation or insight," Deborah continues. "It's not about keeping score. Sometimes you're in a place where you're the one to take ninety percent and give ten percent. Other times, you're the giver. When that happens and someone says 'thank you,' I feel great. Perhaps they made headway because I helped them take a deep breath for a moment. At the end of my life, I will judge myself not by my bank balance or my job title but by the quality of my relationships. There's no better feeling than knowing you had a part in making a positive difference for someone."

Jessica, 32, became friends with two women at the bank where she works. "When we first met, I was twenty years old and they were thirty-five and fifty. They cared for me at work," she says. "I remember one of them asking me, 'Your smile's gone, Jessica. What's not working?' We call ourselves the Pepper Sisters because we gave each other necklaces that look like chili peppers. We are now ages thirty-two, forty-seven, and sixty-two, and even though my older friend retired and moved to Florida, we're all still in contact."

Even in a small office, friends at work make life better. Karen, 52, manages a dental office, and though the technicians are younger by fifteen to twenty years, she feels surrounded by girlfriends all day long. "The girls know all about my husband and sons—both the good and the bad," she says. "They give me grief about the music I like and tease me when my young adult sons call. While we have our moments, most of the time we have a lot of fun. A lot of my social needs are met at work, which is not always good. By the end of the day, I'm ready for some alone time and perhaps could be doing more with other friends. I guess it's all about balance."

For women whose jobs demand travel, having work friends to go out to dinner, shop, or sightsee with makes a difference. "When you travel, you see each other tired and hungry, so you get to know one another pretty well," says Charlene, 43, a program director. "You can only talk about work so long, which means you soon know what work friends really care about. I always find that I have so much in common with them. We go through so many life events together, be it marriages, raising kids, or family members passing. I've had women I work with give me baby clothes one day and a job reference the next. Having friends at work has never backfired on me. I learned early in my career the difference between sharing and gossiping. Don't say something you're not willing to have come back to you."

Social media has made it easier than ever to stay in touch with work colleagues we meet along our career path. "I still am very close to women I worked with fifteen years ago, and social media has helped me do that," says Charlene. "Sites like LinkedIn and Facebook provide a central portal to keep up-to-date on where people are and to have access to what they're doing. It helps us to continue to support one another."

G✳TCHA! MOMENT

Shift Your Paradigm and Step Out with Colleagues

Stumped for what to do with work friends? Here are a dozen ways to get out of the workplace and connect at another level:

1. Treat yourselves to a wine bar and music night.
2. Take in a baseball game and munchies beforehand.
3. See a movie/play and review the performance over coffee.
4. Volunteer together at a food bank or neighborhood cleanup.
5. Support a needy family with a gift basket the team delivers personally.
6. Hold a cookie exchange with enough to take home.
7. Go bowling and enjoy a fifties diner afterward.
8. Rent sailboats or kayaks for a Saturday outing.
9. Make beaded jewelry or shop at a craft fair.
10. Wrap your holiday gifts communally; don't forget the spiked eggnog.
11. Form a team, and enter a charity run.

12. Initiate fun with an e-mail and an event link with a note, "Want to join me?"

Joining Professional Organizations Can Yield Close Friends

Professional associations and organizations are rich venues for developing friendships with like-minded women. Focused on women in business, they provide terrific forums for meeting other professional women and lead to welcome friendships. A circle of peers can help us find our voice and motivate us to action. They offer collective wisdom enabling us to do more and be more than we are on our own.

"I've always taken advantage of networking and professional development groups," says Margie, 70. "I've belonged to PEO (Philanthropic Educational Organization); the sorority, KAPPA; and many others. Whenever I've moved, these kinds of structured groups allowed me to quickly connect with like-minded souls."

When attending professional association meetings, how we show up can make or break our success. What attitude do we bring? Are we receptive or closed off? Do we participate with our heart *and* mind? Are we open to listening to all voices? Keeping these questions in mind allows us to build a network of women who understand what we're going through yet are distant enough from our everyday environment to offer fresh insights and perspectives.

"In a company you have to be careful, and choose friends who can be confidantes," says Deborah, 48. "Unfortunately I've heard many stories about women who have been hurt by other women climbing the corporate ladder. I've been involved in Healthcare Businesswomen's Association for twenty-some years. Because these are not women I work with daily, they've become my closest mentors, coaches, and friends."

Deborah became a founding member of the Atlanta chapter of Healthcare Businesswomen's Association in 1997 to expand her friendship base. "I've met so many women who support me in my career and with whom I have become friends," she says. "I couldn't have achieved what I have without more senior women opening up themselves to be my friends. They were so generous and helped me see that I had as much to offer as they did. Now I help those more junior and make sure I take my title out of the way. It's so worth it because of everything I give and everything I get back."

Jacqueline, 62, spent twenty-five years of her information technology career avoiding connecting with women because she saw it as a sure way to short-change her career. Then she met Amelia at a golf clinic.

"Amelia started talking about a leadership experience she was going to be facilitating with eight professional women in Costa Rica," remembers Jacqueline. "When I went back to work, I courageously approached my boss about sending me on this career opportunity. To this day I don't know what switched in my head that it was OK to go hang out with only women, but it was life altering. The amazing women I met there helped me to understand my special blessings and changed my life in one wonderful week. Now, ten years later, they continue to be my friends and cheerleaders. They help me see the value I offer to the world. I am forever grateful that I took that step to avail myself of this awesome connection with other professional women."

Many companies support business resource groups that foster connection among team members with similar backgrounds, from gender and ethnicity to disabilities and sexual orientation. While all of these groups offer opportunities to develop work friendships, a women's business resource group is especially powerful. These groups focus on the special needs and circumstances faced by women in the workplace. Members often share ideas on how to balance life and work, while forming friendships with women from different departments who may not have otherwise met.

Work-based clubs and classes, such as Toastmasters, book clubs, yoga, or hiking groups also provide entrée to women with common interests. These groups recharge our batteries while igniting new relationships.

Mentor/Mentee Friendships

Mentoring promotes strong bonds among diverse women, often lasting long after the formal mentorship ends. What's important is that each individual feels safe. We can't open our minds and hearts or share our insights and values without mutual respect for the boundaries of the mentorship.

Leesa, 53, who is single, says she has mentored a number of younger professional women who are now some of her best friends.

"We discovered we enjoy each other's company and share some of the same special interests," says Leesa. "We go on walks, take cooking classes, and talk about career challenges. I've learned that we can appreciate each other for who we are. I don't have to pretend to be thirtysomething, and they don't have to act like they're older. And I'm not afraid to joke about being the 'old dog' in the room.

"These women keep me young-minded for sure. Once we've developed a certain level of trust, they talk about their love lives and personal challenges. I can usually say, 'Boy, have I seen that or had a similar experience.' When we're willing to share, it forms a bond. No matter how old we are, the patterns of life are still the same."

Marie, 50, has many mentoring relationships that are still going strong even after the work commitment ended. "The intensity of the work we did together made our relationship really meaningful, and that continued when we transitioned into friendship.

"Today I mentor Jennifer. She's free to call or e-mail me at will. I understand her situation, be it career or personal, and I am happy to share my insight. It's refreshing that she's younger than I am. We learn from each other."

Marie has another mentee through the Foreign Women's Association. She's in her twenties and an accountant with an MBA. Very adventurous, with a love for theater and improv, her special interests turned the table, and Marie became the mentee!

"One day, Aspen invited me to go to an improv theater session," says Marie. "Watching those talented individuals made me realize that having stage presence and thinking on my feet could help me not be so cerebral. We did a show for a full audience, which was such a fun experience. I learned to just go with it, trust my stage mates, accept gifts from them, and build on that…it opened up my mind. The experience made me more flexible to accept my imperfections and to have fun—it was a whole different approach in personal development."

G✳TCHA! MOMENT

Mentorships for Friendships

Being a mentor or mentee is easy when your company has a formal mentorship program, but what if it doesn't? Here are a few ways to create that mentor relationship:

✳ Pick a woman you admire at work. Define what you could learn from her, be it her business acumen or personal style. Then ask her to be your mentor. You might start with an e-mail outlining your goal and outcome for the mentorship. Request a thirty-minute meeting with her. No doubt she'll be flattered. If she declines, ask who she'd recommend.

❋ Check with your professional association or a women's organization to see if it has a formal mentorship program, and sign up to be a mentor or a mentee.

❋ Seek out someone in your profession who has just won a prestigious award. Reach out to see if she'd be willing to share insights with you.

❋ Join a nonprofit board that includes women you admire. Volunteer for assignments to be informally mentored. Invite those you admire to coffee or lunch and learn even more!

Chapter 11

Savoring the Blessings:
Gratitude and Acknowledgment

Next to our health, family, and faith, few things are more valuable than friendship. Friendship is not something we can buy. We can only invest in it and feel the rewards over time. It's a gift given freely and built in moments of grace. Consciously "knowing" how fortunate we are to have committed friendships makes them all the more special.

"The message of intentional friendship moves me to tears," says Barbara, 42, a gift store owner. "In thinking about my good friends and the trials and tribulations we've shared, I realized that making a commitment to being lifelong friends and growing old together is really an important part of our friendship. I'm thankful that I now ask this of my friends."

Knowing that we are not alone or singular in our experiences of life is fundamental for women. Nurturing female friendships is critical to our overall well-being.

"Friends help me turn the pages of my life," says Donna, 67. "When we reach certain stages—whether having children or going through menopause—we need our bearings. Other women give us that just by knowing they are going through similar experiences on this incredible journey."

It's the relatedness and understanding experienced with our friends that's so priceless. Committed relationships bring us the comfort of knowing that someone cares enough to "get us."

"Women connect at a level that doesn't need a lot of explanation," says Lynn, 57. "As friends, we have a predisposed understanding of so many of each other's emotions and experiences. I can't imagine life without my female friends. They allow me to stay young, make me laugh at myself, bring sense to chaos, and are honest enough to tell me what I *need* to hear."

Friends fill us up in a distinct way. Sometimes their presence is all we need to feel better—their words exactly what we long for to feel understood.

"The blessings of friendship allow me to build *muscle memory* of the heart," says Noonie, 51. "Just as I had to practice long hours on the piano to master *Moonlight Sonata*, growing into my own skin has become a little more automatic each day. I owe a lot of this progress to my girlfriends, who have helped fill the space of the larger-than-life spirit of my grandma Iris, who has left this earth but will never leave my heart. She raised me from age two and always made me feel accepted and loved, even in the most trying times. Her optimism, humor, and utterly joyful laugh became my own, and I carry those in me like the most precious treasures. Though I lost her twenty years ago, I still lean on her for advice and perspective, and smile at how she would have handled situations.

"I'm able to keep these memories alive through a close friend who knew my grandma well," continues Noonie. "Both attended my wedding, twenty-five years ago. Grammie referred to us as the 'Awesome Twosome.' Still today when one of us is faced with a challenging moment, we'll often exclaim Grammie's signature phrase, 'It's a great life if you don't weaken!' Somehow it helps us tough it out and stay strong. We send each other cards picturing an iris flower, usually signed "with gratitude," which lightens my day and renews my bond with my treasured friend who has known me—and my story—for more than half my life.

"Girlfriends value the process of learning, growing, and reinventing ourselves together. And they contribute patience as we strive to become our strongest, most graceful, and best selves. I try to make a point to express gratitude to the people who bless my life. It *is* a great life if you don't weaken, and thanks to the great women in my life, I almost never weaken!" Noonie says.

Friends deserve to be handled with care. Recognizing their value and expressing our gratitude are two of the best ways to savor the blessings of friendships. It's imperative to acknowledge how much we appreciate their company, insight, and support. While it's not about keeping things even, chances are when we do let our friends know what they mean to us, we'll hear how much we mean to them in return. Kind words may not come back to us at the exact same moment, but caring friends do reciprocate. Friendship is a circle of giving and receiving, and worth every ounce of effort.

"I like to text my friend Brittney inside jokes," says Amanda, 26. "Since we are both nurses, I occasionally text her about something that happened at work that made me think of her. Or I'll send her a picture with the happy face symbol from somewhere I am that reminds me of her. We have the kind of connection that when we are in a certain situation, we can just look at each other and know exactly what the other is thinking, and it makes us laugh hysterically."

If we're not mindful, we can get stuck on autopilot and take our friends for granted. Acknowledging what our friends mean to us helps avoid future "if onlys." Better to err on the side of generosity than live with regrets. If we're thinking something flattering about our friend, why not say it? If we appreciate a kind gesture, why not let her know? Now is the time to show our friends how much we cherish them, what we admire in them, and the joy they bring to our lives!

Our Cup Overflows

To savor the blessings of friendship, we must intentionally go the extra mile. Be thoughtful, insightful, and kind—and allow others to do the same for us. Accept gestures of gratitude graciously while giving of ourselves abundantly.

To reap the full rewards of friendship, be sensitive and responsive to a friend's true needs. Diane's friend Lolma, 62, has a special gift of insight into others' situations and emotions. She has a knack of saying just the right thing to let a friend know that what she's going through is really important to her. One year, when Diane mentioned that her birthday would be the first since her mom passed away, Lolma did more than say she knew that would be difficult. She asked Diane if she'd like to share a memory of her mother. That simple invitation allowed Diane to remember not only the good times she and her mother shared but who her mother was as a person.

Diane learned an invaluable lesson that day. Rather than responding by rote, taking a few minutes to understand what your friend *really* needs in the moment is a gift we can all give. It costs nothing, and the reward is invaluable. After all, isn't friendship at its best when we work to understand and support each other with a sincere heart?

Liz, 54, who is single and lives alone in Boston, Massachusetts, broke her foot and was housebound for months. Three friends from her annual sailing adventure, each living in different parts of the country, traveled to be with her for a week.

"I'm not good at receiving that kind of love and care…I know how fortunate I am to have that surround me," says Liz.

G✺TCHA! MOMENT

From Feeling Blasé to Blessed

If you feel blasé about a friendship—that it's growing stale, or you're not connecting at the heart the way you once did—check your motives and try these steps. (We're not talking major conflict here; we addressed that in Chapter 7.)

Step one: Free yourself of negative self talk such as, "Why am I the one always making the first move or expressing a gesture of kindness?" or "She must not care as much as I do."

Step two: Imagine what support or kindness your friend may need or want from you at the moment.

Step three: Give from the heart without expecting anything in return. Make the call, send the note, or extend an offer to get together. Everyone likes to know how much she's been missed and the important role she plays in your life.

Authentically Expressing Gratitude

We all like to feel appreciated, and many of us are good at thanking our friends for what they do for us. Let's go a step beyond, and tell our friends how much they *mean* to us. It may seem awkward or like the timing is not quite right. But to our friends, the timing will *always* be perfect.

"One of the great ways to attract positive energy is to express gratitude explicitly," says Charlene, 43. "We might think, 'Of course my friend knows I think she's great, or love her, or will always be here for her.' But why not take away the guesswork and tell her? My dad always said, 'When you're thinking something nice about someone, let them know.' Taking time to tell my friends what they mean to me keeps me connected to the women I want to grow old with. I'm a fan of writing or text messaging to let someone know I am thinking of them. I text, 'How's it going?' or 'Hope you're having a great day.' Yet in our electronic world, handwritten notes are special."

Ellen, 60, goes out of her way to show her friends she cares.

"Thoughtfulness is a dying art," she says. "I like to acknowledge special events in my friends' lives and to remember times we've shared together. When I return from a trip with girlfriends, I invite them to meet for happy hour to share our memories and pictures. We laugh all over again as we relive the experience."

Sometimes kindness shows up in small gestures with big meaning. Ellen told her friend Deb that when she was recovering from cancer surgery, several friends would stop by with Chinese food and fortune cookies. She always put the fortunes in a cookie jar for later.

"One New Year's Eve, when I was all alone and having a pity party, I opened up champagne and picked a cookie from the jar," Ellen told Deb. "It read, 'You discover treasure where others see nothing unusual.' I realized then that's exactly what I do. Clients tell me their stories, and I unearth the golden nuggets to build their brands. A year later for my birthday, Deb gave me a sterling silver fortune cookie keychain. It was so special because she remembered my story and bought me a present that related to it.

"We're each other's cheering section. When I read a story Deb's written for the newspaper, I am the first one to call her and tell her what I loved about her writing. Similarly she goes out of her way to help recruit clients for my 'branding with charisma' workshops. While I'm strong, optimistic, and always helping others, I need to have someone in my life who will let me be a victim from time to time. Deb is a friend who allows me to lean on her when I need it. When someone steps in and helps me, I'm over the moon. I'll jump through hoops for them."

Gifts from the Heart

While sharing kind words is perhaps the most wonderful way to savor the blessings of friendship, it's great to express our appreciation in other meaningful ways. Lolma likes to surprise her friends with gifts from time to time—and not just at the holidays. When she goes out to dinner, she often delights her friends by picking up the bill.

"I also love to send the right card to the right person at the right time," she says. "It makes me feel connected. And I like to keep cards my friends send me. I read these cards when I'm missing them or feeling a bit blue."

Keeping a daily gratitude journal helps us focus on what we have, not what we're lacking. Molly, 58, takes out her gratitude list when she's experiencing a bad day.

"It's amazing to see what my friends have done for me. I go out of my way to cheer up my friends," Molly continues. "I like to put a positive spin on things and remind those close to me to have faith and not live in fear. I remind them that fear is just false evidence appearing real. I also go out of my way to let friends know I care. I send flowers and tell jokes. If I see something they might be interested in, I call to let them know or e-mail a link so they can check it out. Making other people happy brings me great joy. I love to show my love and affection for my friends."

Showing she cares allows Brittany, 32, a financial analyst, to stay plugged in to her friends' lives. "I'm a greeting card junkie," she says. "If I go into a card store for one card, I'll come out with eight. I send them to my friends for a variety of reasons, not necessarily for special occasions. If one of my friends is down, I'll send a note of encouragement. Sending cards is one way I stay in touch. It gives me the opportunity to write something I might not otherwise say. A sentimental message is easier to write on a greeting card than in an e-mail or on Facebook."

Brittany is also big on what she calls "random gifting." "Since I have a lot of friends overseas and don't see them every day, if I see something they'll appreciate, I just send it to them. I have a friend in England whose sister was trying to get pregnant. She considered donating her eggs, because in England a person has to know the donor. Since my friend was on the fence, I bought a bunch of books online and sent them to her. She was so surprised I went to all that trouble."

Once Brittany bought herself a lip gloss at her favorite department store, and she picked up a second tube for a friend. The next time she and her friend were together, she dropped it into her handbag.

"I find joy in giving and never keep track. It's not about reciprocity, and because of that, it makes my relationship with my girlfriends feel like family."

Similarly, Charlene, 43, likes to surprise her friends. "One day I was agonizing about the wrinkles under my eyes, and feeling particularly vulnerable, I bought two bottles of Dead Sea products at the mall kiosk. A few days later, a friend at work was talking about the same thing. So I brought in the product and left it for her with a little note. She was blown away that just out of the blue someone would give her a gift. It felt great!"

Be There for Your Friends: Show Up When It Matters Most

When we put ourselves in our friends' shoes and use thoughtfulness as our guide, it demonstrates, in a concrete way, the significance and value of friendship.

Diane, who experienced being alone again in midlife, has a special place in her heart for single women, especially now that she's married. She thinks about what she would have appreciated when partner-less and stands in their shoes. When her single friend hosted a dinner party for three couples, Diane knew how brave it was to be the only single person at the party. Sensing how lonely it could be cleaning up after everyone left for the evening, she and her husband made sure they did the dishes, especially the pots and pans. The next day her friend sent a text message thanking her for such a kind gesture.

Pat, 65, a communications consultant, believes strongly in the adage, "The only way to have a friend is to be one." With that in mind, she strives to be the best friend she can be, especially during tough times.

"I'll literally drop what I'm doing to counsel a friend by phone, by e-mail, or (when possible) in person. I'm never late for a birthday greeting," she says. "I still send old-fashioned greeting cards and call or do something to celebrate with them. My longtime friend, Gloria, twenty years my senior, has a number of health problems. One year for her birthday, I drove about one hundred miles round trip to see her. I brought her a Mylar "Happy Birthday" balloon and a bottle of wine and then treated her to dinner and a movie. Gloria said that was one of the best birthdays she ever experienced!"

About two months ago, Pat learned that her friend in Michigan lost her husband to a heart attack. Pat immediately called Kathy, sent a sympathy card with a donation, and followed up with several phone calls. When another friend, Lisa, was despondent over losing a job, Pat took time to listen.

A few years ago, when Pat was out of work and hurting for money, her friends Bonnie and Terry sent her a check for $1,000.

"The money was a gift with no strings attached, but a few years later, I paid them back in full. Bonnie supported me when I had breast cancer and has even styled my hair for a job interview—that I got! I'll never forget their generosity.

"Friendships must be reciprocal and authentic. When this happens, not even the most handsome, sexy, or wealthy man can replace those feelings of fulfillment and security."

G✻TCHA! MOMENT

GOTCHA! Moment: Five Fun and Low-Cost Ways to Say, "You Matter, Girl!"

Here are some thoughts for how to recognize and appreciate your friends:

1. Mail a handwritten note acknowledging her kind gestures.
2. Pay your friend a gratitude visit. Pack a picnic basket with wine and chocolates, and then list a dozen ways her presence makes a difference in your life.
3. Appreciate your friend on her Facebook wall by highlighting her special traits. All her friends can share the moment with her.
4. Invite your friend over for lunch, but don't let her bring a thing. Fancy it up with her favorite music and dessert.
5. Take one thing off your friend's to-do list. Pick up her dry cleaning, order something online that she's been putting off, or make cookies for her child's school.

Whatever we do for our friends, the point is to leave them feeling honored and experiencing how much they matter to us. Our friends bring the voice of reason, perspective, and validation. They make us feel better, not worse. They fill our lives with balance and well-being. Good friends bring out our best. With purposeful intention, we will nourish, develop, and grow our circle of female friends. We must grab the opportunity and invite our friends to be women we want to grow old with! Bet they'll ask the same of us!

About the Authors

Diane Gage Lofgren has authored nine books and scores of magazine articles on personal and business relationships. She serves as senior vice president and chief communication officer for a national health care organization.

Margaret Bhola has an extensive background in nutrition, business, sales and marketing, and human relations. She became a top national sales producer for several large companies and is known as an effective leader and team coach.

Made in the USA
San Bernardino, CA
05 January 2015